PHOTOGRAPHY YEAR

PHOTOGRAPHY YEAR
1979 EDITION
BY THE EDITORS OF TIME-LIFE BOOKS

TIME-LIFE BOOKS, ALEXANDRIA, VIRGINIA

The Library of Congress Cataloged This Serial
as Follows:
TR1   Photography year.
.P8819 New York, Time-Life Books.
         v.   illus.   26cm.   annual
         1. Photography-Yearbooks   I. Time-Life Books
TR 1. P8819   770'.5   72-91518
ISSN 0090-4406   MARC-S
Library of Congress   73[2]

ON THE COVER: An old-fashioned, romantic portrait of a Spanish señorita and the loudspeaker-microphone of a new automatic focusing system based on sound represent two of 1978's photographic achievements. The hand-colored picture of the lady with the fan is the work of newly discovered talents, two brothers from Barcelona, Ramón and Antón Eguiguren. The gold-colored disc, part of Polaroid's Sonar SX-70 camera, bounces a high-frequency chirp of sound off the subject to measure its distance from the camera, then turns the lens to focus at that distance. Beside the disc is an electronic pattern recording one complete sonic cycle, from the moment the chirp emerges from the camera until it returns in a flurry of vibrations before dying out.

Contents

Time-Life Books Inc.
is a wholly owned subsidiary of

TIME INCORPORATED

FOUNDER: Henry R. Luce 1898-1967

Editor-in-Chief: Hedley Donovan
Chairman of the Board: Andrew Heiskell
President: James R. Shepley
Vice Chairmen: Roy E. Larsen, Arthur Temple
Corporate Editors: Ralph Graves, Henry Anatole Grunwald

TIME-LIFE BOOKS INC.

MANAGING EDITOR: Jerry Korn
Executive Editor: David Maness
Assistant Managing Editors: Dale M. Brown (planning),
George Constable, Jim Hicks (acting), Martin Mann,
John Paul Porter
Art Director: Tom Suzuki
Chief of Research: David L. Harrison
Director of Photography: Robert G. Mason
Senior Text Editor: Diana Hirsh
Assistant Art Director: Arnold C. Holeywell
Assistant Chief of Research: Carolyn L. Sackett
Assistant Director of Photography: Dolores A. Littles

CHAIRMAN: Joan D. Manley
President: John D. McSweeney
Executive Vice Presidents: Carl G. Jaeger,
John Steven Maxwell, David J. Walsh
Vice Presidents: Peter G. Barnes (Comptroller),
Nicholas Benton (Public Relations), John L. Canova
(Sales), Nicholas J. C. Ingleton (Asia), James L. Mercer
(Europe/South Pacific), Herbert Sorkin (Production),
Paul R. Stewart (Promotion)
Personnel Director: Beatrice T. Dobie
Consumer Affairs Director: Carol Flaumenhaft

EDITORIAL STAFF FOR PHOTOGRAPHY YEAR

EDITOR: Edward Brash
Picture Editor: Adrian Allen
Text Editor: Betsy Frankel
Chief Researcher: Juanita James Wilson
Assistant Designer: Edwina C. Smith
Staff Writer: Susan Feller
Researchers: Fran Ahders, Karen Bates-Logan,
Jeremy N. P. Ross, David J. Schrieberg, B. Jean Strong
Editorial Assistant: Janet Doughty

Editorial Production
Production Editor: Douglas B. Graham
Operations Manager: Gennaro C. Esposito,
Gordon E. Buck (assistant)
Assistant Production Editor: Feliciano Madrid
Quality Control: Robert L. Young (director), James J. Cox
(assistant), Michael G. Wight (associate)
Art Coordinator: Anne B. Landry
Copy Staff: Susan B. Galloway (chief), Peter Kaufman,
Cynthia Kleinfeld, Celia Beattie
Picture Department: Sara Schneidman
Traffic: Jeanne Potter

*Portions of this book were written by Don Earnest,
James A. Randall and John von Hartz.*

Correspondents: Elisabeth Kraemer (Bonn); Margot
Hapgood, Dorothy Bacon (London); Susan Jonas, Lucy
T. Voulgaris (New York); Maria Vincenza Aloisi,
Josephine du Brusle (Paris); Ann Natanson (Rome).
Valuable assistance was also provided by: Nina
Lindley (Buenos Aires); Peter Hawthorne
(Johannesburg); Diane Asselin (Los Angeles); Bill
Lyon (Madrid); Bernard Diederich, Pedro Meyer (Mexico
City); Felix Rosenthal (Moscow); Carolyn T. Chubet,
Miriam Hsia (New York); Dag Christensen (Oslo); Alison
Raphael, Mark Gruberg (Rio de Janeiro); Janet
Huseby (San Francisco); Jane Baird (San Juan); Peter
Allen (Sydney); Parvis Raein (Tehran); Ken Bloom
(Tokyo).

The private concerns of the artist—for form, color and, above all, for self-expression—captured the eye of photography's public in 1978 as never before. Simultaneously, developments in cameras, lenses and films that are revolutionizing photography promised even greater freedom for the artist in pursuit of his esthetic goals.

The news in technology may prove to have the greatest long-range impact. High-speed slide film and fast, inexpensive plastic lenses were introduced, enabling any photographer to take hand-held color pictures anywhere without using flash. Automatic exposure is now controlled by built-in computers that make cameras almost think for themselves. And, in two instant-picture cameras, beams of inaudible sound waves focus lenses automatically. For many amateurs, these improvements do away with the nuisances of dial-setting, needle-matching and focusing. For serious photographers they eliminate mechanical constraints that get in the way of artistic goals.

The personal nature of art was obvious in one of 1978's most talked-about shows, the Museum of Modern Art's survey of recent American photography. But private concerns also were evident in less publicized exhibits. New galleries around the world were providing more wall space for emerging artist-photographers, and many of these same photographers were receiving an increasing amount of no-strings-attached financial support from corporations, governmental agencies and foundations to pursue their image-making.

The emphasis on self-expression also surfaced in one of the year's best books, an anthology of 119 photographs by women using the camera to probe the female psyche. And in Chicago, stunning portraits and self-portraits were the result of a community program in which students were being taught how to use the camera as a tool for self-expression.

Most notable of all, however, were the decidedly subjective leanings of the three Americans and a team of Spanish brothers whose work was chosen in *Photography Year*'s 1978 worldwide hunt for unrecognized talent. Each of the year's newcomers is as intent as any painter on conveying personal visions. Two already are testing the limits of the new color film. One shoots in the evening twilight; the other takes pictures in the middle of the night.

The Editors

Trends/1

Trends/1

U.S.A. — Various Gifts and Grants

This 97-year-old woman, a former suffragette, is one of many residents from old working-class communities in East Baltimore, Maryland, that photography teacher Linda Rich and two of her students, Joan Netherwood and Elinor Cahn, photographed for a documentary project begun in 1976. The project, funded by some 40 public and private sources, is described in an article beginning on page 38 that details the sharp increase in grants for photographers.

Bankrolling Photographers/ LINDA RICH: *Mrs. Virginia Jensen, 1977*

A Youthful New Wave in Photography

Supplied with inexpensive cameras and inspired instruction, young people are surprising their elders with pictures of power and beauty

Images of poignant power frozen by the camera's lens, pictures that capture a moment of drama, that seize the eye and the mind with unusual composition, that make cunning use of light and shadow, that record human personalities with honesty and subtle humor—such are the qualities of a surprising body of photographs produced not by professional photographers but by unsophisticated amateurs. Most were taken by youngsters, some of whom are still in elementary school, many of whom are poor, and most of whom have had little opportunity to express themselves at all, let alone with a camera. In one case (pages 24-25), the striking pictures are one adult's successful effort to substitute visual communication for speech.

The photographers were all participants in a variety of 1978 educational and social programs aimed at putting cameras into the hands of novices. There were about 500 such efforts, new or continuing, in the United States alone, as well as scores of others in Italy, Scotland, Canada and South Africa. Materials and funds for the courses came from government agencies and private sources, including several manufacturers of photographic equipment.

Although these undertakings were designed to introduce young people to the pleasures of successful picturetaking and the praise that goes with it, they varied in their emphasis, depending upon the particular situation and the philosophies of the teachers. Some emphasized the techniques of the camera and darkroom, while others stressed the resulting photograph. One teacher in a poor neighborhood in Puerto Rico said that among his students, just owning and knowing how to use a camera was a matter of pride and prestige.

Like teaching devices of any sort—pencils, crayons, paints—the camera was a useful tool in helping students articulate their thoughts. An instructor in Chicago had students make self-portraits, then study their pictures and talk on the subject: "Who am I deep inside?" A teacher in a coal-mining district of Kentucky took students into the mines with their cameras to "explore more closely their own lives and unique culture."

In many communities, the public recognition that can be achieved by students' work is a major goal. Student photographs have appeared in art shows and even in major museums, and a nonprofit group in Puerto Rico used student photographs to produce its own calendar. One of the picturetaking trips of the children in the Kentucky program was filmed and featured on a national television show. As a result of this attention, the courses themselves are gaining recognition as a significant force in education. In preparation is the Bulletin for Community Photographic Education, a newsletter designed to link together this array of photography programs for young people. According to the Bulletin's creators, photographers Tom Sherman and Susan Rosenberg, themselves teachers in a children's program in Delaware, the publication will serve as a news and information clearinghouse for the network of teachers and administrators who are engaged in similar work.

Meanwhile, the programs are proliferating as fast as film and cameras can be purchased and distributed to students—and in some cases, as fast as suitable space can be found for darkrooms. Although many programs rely on inexpensive cameras and drugstore processing, several also teach developing and printing. In already overcrowded schools, this sometimes requires drastic measures: one determined group in Markham, Illinois, set up its enlargers on the toilet lids in a high-school washroom. Such determination attests to the interest aroused in students. And the proof of the success of the programs can be seen in their pictures.

Harry Mangual, a 12-year-old student of the Playa de Ponce Photography Workshop, took this picture of some fellow students—two of them with their cameras hanging around their necks—sailing into some fast food as they go for a stroll down a residential street in the seaport town of Ponce, Puerto Rico.

The list at right describes a group of photography courses for children representative of the hundreds of such programs around the world. Instruction and materials for courses such as these are free to the students, many of whom are poor or so geographically isolated that they have never seen a camera.

PHOTOGRAPHY COURSES FOR CHILDREN	
Apeiron Millerton, New York Peter Schlessinger, director	One-day to one-week class of photography instruction in rural elementary and high schools
Children's Photographic Workshop Salt Lake City, Utah Brent Herridge, director	Basics of photography for children in local public schools, on a nearby Navajo Indian reservation and in juvenile-detention centers
Film Workshop Trust Edinburgh, Scotland David Halliday, director	Basics of photography for public-school students and deaf children in special schools
Foto/gram Milan, Italy Ando Gilardi, leader	Photography used to help teach other subjects, such as history and mathematics. Children make shadow images on photographic paper without cameras
Instituto Technico Medici Del Vascello; Liceo Scientifico J. F. Kennedy Rome, Italy Gabriele Morrione, director	Camera techniques and photography criticism for high-school students
International Center of Photography New York, New York Via Wynroth, education director	Community workshops in photography plus courses at the Center in special subjects such as color printing and darkroom technique
Langa, South Africa Bob Denton, director/teacher	Basics of photography, taught in a local church
Les Rochelais Voient Leur Vie Dans La Ville La Rochelle, France Claude Raymond-Dityvon, director	Demonstrations and instruction by the director, a professional photographer, for beginners

Young Eyes' Images

Some of the most professional-looking photographs produced by the burgeoning programs for children come from unlikely places—dirt-poor districts, rural and urban, such as the section of the port city of Ponce, Puerto Rico, called Playa de Ponce. Here 64 youths are busily making pictures, among warehouses, docks and the rusted hulks of cars that litter the beach, in a photography program at a community center run by nuns and volunteers.

The work of teenagers like Carmen Santos, two of whose luminous portraits of young friends appear at right and on page 16, manages to convey a sense of beauty in squalor. However, beautiful photographs are not the principal goal of the program. Rather, it strives to instill a sense of self-esteem in children whose poverty-stricken lives give them few opportunities to win acclaim for achievements. In this purpose, the program has been hugely successful. The students have seen their pictures reproduced commercially, and even exhibited in New York City's Metropolitan Museum of Art.

A young boy fingering a makeshift toy looks up for this pensive portrait taken by Carmen Santos, age 16, on the stone stairs of an elementary school.

A sand-encrusted section of concrete pipe provides
a playground for Puerto Rican youths —and a curving
frame for this picture by 17-year-old Antonio Zayas.

Natural light, bathing this little girl at her chores, turns her hair into a glowing halo. This picture by Carmen Santos, like the one on page 14, resulted from an assignment to record life in the barrio that is her home.

Caught as he dozed with glasses held precariously in one hand, an elderly fruit seller outside his stand is swallowed by shadows in this photograph, which was taken by 15-year-old Edwin Santiago.

An assignment to take photographs of New Yorkers at work resulted in this picture by Rolando Santiago, age 16, of a fireman trainee wrestling to get a faulty hose under control while instructors in the background impassively observe his performance.

The Child's View of New York

Nestled between public housing projects and tenements on Manhattan's Lower East Side, the nonprofit Henry Street School is part of the Henry Street Settlement, an 85-year-old community agency that originated as a visiting-nurse service for immigrants from Eastern Europe.

In 1970 the settlement, whose programs have grown and altered with changes in the neighborhood population, introduced a photography course for children. Nancy Starrels, who currently conducts the class, teaches students such basic camera operations as setting f-stops and focusing, then takes them on field trips to explore—and photograph—places in New York City they would not ordinarily see.

On one assignment, Starrels' students spent a day on an island in New York's East River photographing a firemen's training center normally off limits to the public. Students can also pursue individual interests—one youngster devoted to bodybuilding hung out at a local gym with his camera for several days taking pictures of musclemen.

A brawny bodybuilder uses the roof of a Manhattan tenement for practice in this portrait by Alex Martinez, a 15-year-old Henry Street student. He took the picture while photographing a group of athletes who call themselves The Gladiators.

A Portrait of Appalachia

Simple assignments that focus upon familiar subjects make up the course taught by 27-year-old photographer Wendy Ewald, who wants her students to record their impressions of the world that surrounds them in eastern Kentucky's Appalachian Mountains. For example, children from the one-room Kingdom Come School and the Cowan School in Letcher County were asked to make pictures of members of their immediate families. On another occasion, they were sent to photograph their parents' places of work. One result of this trip is the picture at far right, taken inside a coal mine by a 12-year-old.

Two tots playing on a country road near their home have abandoned their tricycle for the pleasure of wading in a mud puddle. The children are the brother and sister of photographer Bonnie Capps, 12, who had been given a class assignment to photograph her family.

A mile inside a mountain in eastern Kentucky, coal
miners, illuminated by light from the photographer's flash
cube, crouch under the four-foot-high ceiling of a
damp tunnel as they inspect equipment. For sixth-grader
Pam Brashears, it was the first trip inside a mine. For
protection during this dangerous assignment, she and
her classmates were required to don coal-miners'
helmets and carry portable respirators.

A boy dressed in T-shirt and trunks leans against the wall overlooking a YMCA pool in Chicago. The picture was taken by 16-year-old high-school student Donna Ray, who declares that "the main thing I've learned at the Public Art Workshop is to photograph what I see, not what I'm supposed to see."

Images of the Inner City

Simple, strong and direct, the portraits of the inner-city children reproduced on these pages were taken by students of the Public Art Workshop Photography Center on Chicago's west side. For three years under the direction of photographer Jerry Zbiral, PAW put cameras into the hands of 300 children from Chicago's poorest section. Funds for the cameras and for the center's darkroom equipment came from an auction of photographs donated by 135 photographers, including such well-known professionals as Aaron Siskind and the late Minor White.

One student, the center's only adult, used photography in a very special way: he was helped to compensate for a speech problem by learning to "talk" with his camera. His intensely personal pictures appear on pages 24 and 25.

Framed by the bold strip on the wall behind her and the bannister in the foreground, 11-year-old Andrea McCline stands in the stair well of her family home. Although the shutter was tripped by her cousin, Andrea herself aimed and focused the camera, and considers the result a self-portrait.

Chicago's "Picture Man"

Thirty-year-old Ralph Mitchell is one of the great success stories of the Public Art Workshop in Chicago. Followed by flocks of neighborhood children who call him Picture Man, Mitchell roams the streets of Chicago like a latter-day Pied Piper, using secondhand cameras to produce photographs of startling originality.

Often Mitchell uses his friends and neighbors for subjects, and after the film is processed he returns with the prints in hand to share the results with the people he has photographed. In this way Mitchell, who has difficulty speaking, uses his cameras to communicate what he cannot verbalize.

The power evident in Mitchell's pictures is the result, says PAW cofounder Alan Teller, of a "sophisticated and peculiar use of space and a highly personal way of juxtaposing people and places." This gift is obvious in most of Mitchell's pictures, and especially so in the strange scene at right.

A routine occurrence in Chicago—the raising of a drawbridge near an "El" station in the Loop—was shot from an unexpected angle, making the bridge appear to cut across the picture like a giant blade.

This impromptu portrait of a curler-clad friend and
her young daughter owes much of its easy intimacy to the
fact that the photographer's neighbors are
accustomed to his unannounced visits for picturetaking.

Comeback of the Magazines

For inventive, aggressive photojournalists, a boom in magazines that emphasize photographs provides a new market, short on pay but long on opportunities

by Thomas Dickey

Thomas Dickey, a freelance writer, has contributed articles on photography to books and magazines.

When *Look* magazine folded in 1971 and *Life* stopped weekly publication a year later, many people believed that an era was over, that photojournalism had come to a dead end. No more would there be multipage picture essays for staff photographers to shoot; for freelancers the outlook was even gloomier. "I really thought," says photographer Mary Ellen Mark, "that television was the new journalistic medium." But in 1978 there were signs that the death notices had been premature. One of the brightest tidings was the revival of both *Life* and *Look,* which promised once again to provide markets for the best in magazine photography. Beyond that, the magazine field in general was looking up. According to the Audit Bureau of Circulations, a service that monitors every major consumer magazine, the number of magazines rose from 280 in 1973 to 362 in the first half of 1978. During the same period, circulation increased from 259 million issues per month to 316 million.

The result is a rapidly growing, lucrative market for photographers to exploit. But it is a different market from the one that existed in the golden days now gone. Cushy staff jobs are a luxury of the past. But opportunities abound for freelancers—provided they can fulfill the demanding requirements for speed and self-reliance that the magazines of the new era insist on.

The renaissance of photojournalism can be attributed, in part at least, to one cause of its previous decline: television. As commercial space on television has become scarce and expensive (as much as $120,000 for 30 seconds of air time in 1978), advertisers have turned back to the cheaper space found on the magazine page. But the American magazine field—especially the field of picture magazines—has also been stimulated by the continuing popularity of magazines abroad, in Japan, France, Germany, Italy and Brazil. Indeed, the new *Look* is coming to America courtesy of French publisher Daniel Filipacchi, who in 1976 bought and revamped France's pictorial weekly, *Paris-Match,* allotting two thirds of its editorial space to photographs. "It is the renaissance of photography, I would say even the birth of photography for the larger public," says Filipacchi. "There has never before been such great interest in pictures."

Also coming to America from Europe early in 1979 is one of photojournalism's rising new stars, the German monthly, *Geo.* Launched in 1976, *Geo* has joined two popular picture weeklies, *Bunte* and *Stern,* in making Germany one of the outstanding markets for magazine photography. *Geo*'s format of six 20- to 30-page stories an issue on exotic people and places, each accompanied by as many as 25 large four-color photographs, has made the magazine an immediate success: in 1978 its circulation was 331,000. French and Spanish editions have been planned, along with the American entry, and all of them will generate at least three quarters of their own stories, to be photographed by freelancers. This means that the American *Geo* will be providing work for four or five freelance photographers per issue.

As *Geo* tries to establish itself in the United States, it will be competing with the venerable *National Geographic,* one of the few American magazines that have

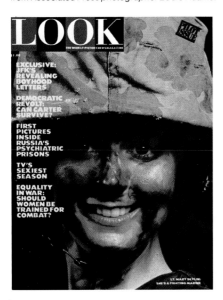

Covers for the reborn Life and Look herald changes
in the market for photojournalism. Like most
of today's magazines, both publications acquire
pictures from outsiders instead of staffers. Life's
balloon picture came from freelancer David Deahl,
Look's shot of Marine Lieutenant Mary Devlin
from Associated Press photographer Eddie Adams.

continued to provide photographers with substantial assignments—that is, those that may involve weeks and even months of work. The *Geographic* has been appealing to a specialized audience since 1888, which makes it in a sense the forerunner of several new special-interest magazines that have moved into the vacuum created by the collapse of the mass-market weeklies. The new magazines, designed for limited but dedicated readership, are rarely affected by television, and they are less economically vulnerable than the old weeklies because they have smaller staffs and lower overhead. As a group they tend to be picture-oriented.

There is, for example, the flourishing *Smithsonian,* which fills roughly half its editorial space with photographs, and the older *Natural History,* which has doubled its budget for photography to $4,500 per issue since 1972, as its readership has surged from 290,000 toward the half-million mark. Other special-interest magazines that emphasize photographs either routinely or occasionally are *Sports Illustrated, Ebony, Ms., Rolling Stone* and *Quest.* For an average issue *Quest* hands out eight assignments, each of them occupying a photographer for one to four days. Furthermore, its editors consider photography so important to the magazine's message, "the pursuit of excellence," that they set aside one or two days a week to review portfolios and evaluate written story proposals from photographers. One indication of *Quest*'s respect for photography is its rates: In 1978 it paid $500 for a full-page black-and-white or color picture, roughly double the amount paid by most other magazines.

In addition to the magazines that cater to special fields of interest is a rapidly growing new group concentrating on particular areas of the country, the so-called regional magazines. Virtually unknown a decade ago, regionals are a '70s publishing phenomenon, and are heavily oriented toward photography. In Texas alone, Dallas has its *D,* Houston its *City,* San Antonio its *SA;* and the entire state is served by the Austin-based *Texas Monthly,* whose quarter-million readers include at least 20,000 Lone Star loyalists living in other states. The prototype for *Texas Monthly* and several other successful regionals is *New York,* which has, since its introduction in 1968, relied more and more on picture stories. *New York*'s deadlines are hard to meet: Most assignments are last-minute affairs and some are due the same day. But the magazine varies its photographic styles; it may employ slick, large-format photography for a food story, but when it carried a feature on New York City's cocaine wars the illustrations were blurry enlargements from a wrist-mounted 35mm Tessina spy camera. *New York* is very receptive to new ideas and new faces. Some of the magazine's best photographic prospects walk in off the street armed only with a portfolio or a story idea.

All of these magazines use color as well as black-and-white photography. As Tom Curtis, editor of Houston's *City,* points out, most of the regionals were started as alternatives to the drab gray of the daily newspaper, so there was always an emphasis on visuals.

But color is also changing the appearance of newspapers. In fact, color has been the principal manner in which a number of newspapers and newsmagazines have upgraded their photography. *The New York Times*, the *Boston Herald American*, the *Los Angeles Herald-Examiner* and *The Washington Post* now use color to glamorize their Sunday magazines, and on the national level *Time* and *Newsweek*, neither of which had more than four color pages a week prior to 1977, have greatly expanded their use of color photography. *Time* now runs eight pages a week, *Newsweek* 13. Furthermore, says *Newsweek* photo editor Jim Kenney, "With color, the trend is to make more assignments than we did in black-and-white, to run more pictures and to run them larger."

Color, in effect, has transformed a number of word magazines into picture magazines. Alice George, former assistant picture editor of *Time*, says the magazine's willingness to spend more money for pictures, to purchase higher-quality printing, to devote more space to photographs in general, was a response to the public's thirst for informative images. Bearing this out is the greatest new market of all for photography: the personality magazine, whose most dynamic resource is the photograph of a public figure. In Europe magazines of this type are booming. The Netherlands has five celebrity magazines, all of them introduced since 1974; their combined readership—in a country of 14,000,000 people—is 1,450,000. In the Americas there is *Fatos e Fotos* in Brazil and, most notably, *People* and *Us* in the United States. Their specialized needs have created opportunities for sophisticated celebrity pictures (for examples, see the picture essay starting on page 30), and those needs at times seem to be insatiable. *People* publishes more than 100 black-and-white photographs each week, which makes it the largest weekly publisher of magazine photographs in the country. Working with a budget that has doubled in four years' time, *People* by 1978 was acquiring 90 per cent of its photographs on commission, was handing out some 25 assignments a week—and had increased its day rates from $150 to $200.

Although the market is much brighter than it was a few years ago, most photographers agree that breaking into it is not easy. There is a lot of competition and, as West Coast photographer Tony Costa puts it, "You have to hustle and show you have ideas." Ideas and inventiveness—the ability to catch exciting and unusual shots even more, perhaps, than artistically composed ones—are what editors look for. And speed.

Few editors today are willing to go over a story explaining what they want, and then underwrite many days of shooting to get it. When photographer John Dominis served as picture editor of *People*, from 1974 to April 1978, he prepped his photographers only for the most complicated assignments. Normally he simply gave them the subject and the gist of the story, and let them take it from there. He expected them to do their own setups and on-location lighting, and he expected them to complete an assignment in a day or two—perhaps in a few hours, if the subject was a famous person.

The photographers who work to these new journalistic standards have to be both

After Moro: Exclusive Interview With Oriana Fallaci
Get Set for Summer: A Guide to Air-Conditioner Tune-Ups

NEW YORK

Say Hallelujah!
New Yorkers Are Being Born Again

Assigned to photograph urban born-again Christians in "baptismal attitudes" for a cover of New York magazine (above), freelancer Ken Ambrose hired models, got a permit to shoot them in a lake in Central Park, briefed costume stylists and spent four hours shooting—all in three days. Fast-working photographers, like Ambrose, who can create seemingly candid scenes are much in demand for assignments on the heavily pictorial magazines launched in the past five years.

quick-witted and resourceful. If they need realistic-looking, candid pictures, they get them any way they can, often posing a setup to appear candid. On a recent two-day assignment to photograph U.S. Congressman Benjamin Gilman, Raeanne Rubenstein spent one day traveling with Gilman in his camper around his district in upper New York state, and a second day recording his daily routine in Washington, D.C. After trailing him around Capitol Hill for several hours, she told him she wanted some pictures of him in his bachelor apartment. "We walked in the door, and the bed was pulled out. He started to fold it up, trying to make the place look neater, but I said, 'Don't, that's perfect.' I had him lie down on it, take off his shoes and read a newspaper—exactly as he would do later that evening. Then, though it was five o'clock in the afternoon, I moved my lights into the kitchen and photographed him making himself a little breakfast. Both those situations captured, I think, the lonely, unglamorous side of this man's life."

Not all such assignments go so smoothly. When Rubenstein photographed Muhammad Ali in his New York City hotel room, she had to compete for his attention with a retinue of his associates. And after she had shot only 10 frames, one of the associates pulled the plug on her lights, abruptly ending the photo session. "Occasions like that," she observes, "have taught me to make every picture count." Similarly, when Tony Costa did an intimate picture story on conductor Zubin Mehta's last days with the Los Angeles Philharmonic before moving to New York, he had to cover one of Mehta's final concerts with a single roll of film. "I wasn't able to reload during the performance because it would have created too much disturbance, so I had to select the shots carefully. I must have had my eye to the finder constantly for 40 minutes."

Like Rubenstein, many of the photographers working for the new magazines are still in their twenties and have only started pursuing their careers in the last half-dozen years. One reason the market has opened up for them is that the established photojournalists, some of whom once earned as much as $100,000 a year from magazines alone, cannot afford to take today's assignments when they can make four times the magazine rate doing advertising photography. Also, as veteran photojournalist Lawrence Fried observes, assignments for the new magazines "never seem to stretch more than two pages or last more than a day or two. It's been years," says Fried, who is now one of the directors of Image Bank, an agency for top advertising and editorial photographers, "since an editor for a magazine other than *Geographic* said to a photographer, 'Take a summer to shoot a definitive story on Iceland or a story on capitalism in Argentina.' Clearly, the photojournalism market has changed drastically."

For the young generation of photojournalists, this change is full of promise. "I'm wondering," says Raeanne Rubenstein, "how the parameters of people photography can be pushed further. It will be interesting to see how photographers trained to this situation will respond when they get assignments for longer pieces from magazines like *Geo* and the new *Life* and *Look*."

A Rage for People Pictures

The kind of photojournalism that makes the new picture magazines so provocative and successful focuses on people's personalities, and goes after pictures that catch their subjects in private moments or revealing situations. To get such pictures, today's photojournalists must exercise a variety of talents—not all of them technical, as the sampling on these pages shows.

Knowing the right people, gaining access to the places where celebrities play, is probably talent number one. When the place is public, like a discotheque, access is relatively easy. But for private parties, nothing helps as much as being a card-carrying member of the "in" group.

For some kinds of celebrity pictures, a talent for voyeurism and a telephoto lens are essential. Other approaches call for the use of makeshift props, and even for skill at getting celebrities to act out scenes from their private lives.

Swiss photographer Ghislaine Morel had the good luck to be close to Prince Charles when the heir to the British Crown decided to sample the samba with dancer Beiza Flor during a fete in his honor in Rio. The picture was published in the Italian magazine Oggi.

The inaugural of a Paris discotheque, the Palace, brought everyone from couturier Yves St. Laurent to the Baron de Rothschild and singer Elton John, offering a field day for cameras. Among the photographers who are represented in this spread from Paris-Match are several who specialize in celebrity-snapping.

At ease with Washington, D.C., insider Diana Walker, reporter Sally Quinn and Presidential assistant Hamilton Jordan merrily hammed it up for the camera when a colleague asked the way to the bathroom at a private Georgetown party. The picture was used in the normally unpictorial New Republic.

Marie-Hélène de Rothschild et le baron Guy.

Un démon irrésistible : Dominique Sanda.

Sous ce masque d'Ange Blanc, Chazot dit-on.

Sorcière au balai-brosse : Paloma Picasso.

Le beau monde y joue à imiter le vilain

Au Palace on se déguise. Loubards et paumés de banlieue se costument en punks, ou en n'importe quoi. Ce sont les nouveaux Incroyables. Il y a heureusement des Merveilleuses. Quant au beau monde qui vient généralement regarder, il arrive qu'à l'occasion d'une soirée organisée par un couturier, il se déguise aussi et rivalise d'extravagances vestimentaires avec le petit peuple des rêveuses banlieues.

Elton John : un diable perché sur talons hauts.

Yves Saint-Laurent : il a patronné la soirée.

Joseph Losey et Madame : comme au cinéma

David de Rothschild et Olympia : au paradis.

A press pass from Manhattan's Soho Weekly News, plus friends on the inside, gained Sonia Moskowitz entry to a publisher's party at a New York discotheque, where she spotted aging enfants terribles Norman Mailer and Truman Capote arm-in-arm. Time magazine picked up the picture.

To symbolize his rigorous training for a 27-city tour, rock musician Udo Jürgens wore a warm-up suit for this ebullient portrait by Manfred Bockelmann. The picture was taken on one day's notice for the German magazine Bunte, to illustrate an article on Jürgens' successful return from semiretirement.

Offbeat Images

Juxtaposing people with campy props or persuading them to assume gimmicky poses is one way to create arresting images of people whose faces may have become too familiar to the general public—and to editors of picture magazines. The best of these unexpected portraits are not only intriguing pictorially; they also shed light on some facet of the subject's personality.

Ordinarily brusque with photographers, Italian film director Federico Fellini agreed to make up as a clown for this set of pictures by Franco Pinna. Pinna, before his death in 1978 (page 235), was the only photographer always welcomed by Fellini on his sets. The pictures have appeared in several magazines; here they accompany an interview with Fellini that ran in Euro.

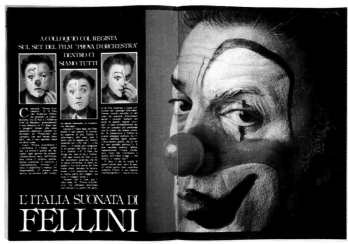

Assigned by People magazine to get a picture of Billy Carter sitting on a throne of beer cans, Atlanta-based photographer Jay B. Leviton rented a motel room in Plains, Georgia, arranged for 26 cases of beer to be delivered there, then constructed this precarious edifice while Billy took a nap on the motel-room sofa.

Neil Leifer's portrait of 18-year-old jockey Steve Cauthen for the cover of Time was taken before Cauthen had actually completed the triple win—Kentucky Derby, Preakness, Belmont Stakes—that earned him the magazine's cover story. To symbolize the expected triumph, Leifer posed the baby-faced Cauthen smiling broadly and smoking a big, expensive cigar.

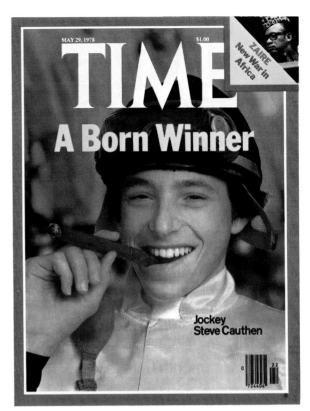

Billy Carter

HE MAY BE A ROYAL PAIN TO SOME, BUT HIS BIG BROTHER IS STILL AMUSED

The bubbling, bumbling, babbling, bibbling sibling of the 39th U.S. President is a King in more than one peanut patch. Billy the Kidder may look like a sack of yams, guzzle beer in the back room of his gas station, tool around in a big white pickup that says REDNECK POWER on the fenders and AIN'T APOLOGIZIN' on the tailgate, and laugh at his own jokes like a mule in the dry heaves. Don't be fooled. Billy is what's known in the South as a Sly Ole Boy.

He sensed from the first that when the horse's mouth wasn't open, the media would gladly listen to the jackass. So he offered himself as the clown prince of the sobersided Carter regime. "I ain't the Carter that don't tell a lie," he brayed happily. "I'll lie like hell in a minute, but I ain't humble worth a damn." The act caught on. Pretty soon the morning mail was bringing Billy about 50 invitations a day.

Now Billy wasn't exactly destitute—he had a right smart income from the family peanut business—but it wasn't in his nature to run under a tree when it was raining money. He hired a bigtime Nashville agent. At $5,000 a shot he appeared at Miss Piggy's Pizza Beauty Pageant in Boston, at the Pole Climbing World Championship in Lexington, Tenn., at the annual World Belly Flop and Cannonball Diving Championship in Vancouver, B.C. For sizable royalties he agreed to endorse a Redneck Power Pickup Truck and Model Kit for Revell.

Then, for an even bigger slice, Billy donated his name to a new product called Billy Beer. It is selling strong in 21 states. "Who knows?" says Billy. "Maybe I'll become the Colonel Sanders of beer."

He is already the Aga Khan of presidential brothers. In 1977, from appearances and endorsements alone, he will earn about $500,000. "I'm sure I'll make more than Jimmy makes"—two and a half times more, to be precise—"but then I work harder," Billy says.

How does the President feel about little brother? White House aides refuse to discuss the matter, but Carter is resolutely making light of it. "I was hoping," he told a Democratic fund-raising dinner in Los Angeles, "that you would raise enough money to have my brother Billy come out and speak next year." □

Billy blithely answers complaints that he is shaming his brother: "There's 150 million times more beer drinkers than there is Presidents."

Photograph by Leviton/Atlanta

Much photographed and completely at ease in front of cameras, country singer Dolly Parton hopped lightheartedly into a tub-turned-trough in a pasture near her home to give photographer Slick Lawson this playful portrait, used by People and Us magazines.

33

Unwelcome Advances

Guts, gall and a hunter's knowledge of his prey are the prime ingredients of the classic *paparazzi* shot—a style once the exclusive specialty of Italian photographers who descend like locusts on their subjects to photograph them against their wishes. Because the subject is usually uncooperative, sometimes aggressively so, the problem is to convert a negative response into an interesting picture.

JACK NICHOLSON FA L'ESIBIZIONISTA

« MI METTO IN POSA »

L'ALTRA FACCIA DEL "CUCULO"

« VI E' PIACIUTO? »

Saint Tropez (Costa Azzurra). Reduce dai trionfi di Taormina, Jack Nicholson deve essersi sentito troppo sicuro di sé, arrivando in Francia, per imbarcarsi sul panfilo del produttore Sam Spiegel. Dal motoscafo, l'attore dell'Oscar (per il film "Qualcuno volò sul nido del cuculo"), ha offerto ai fotografi uno "scatto" veramente eccezionale: la visione dei suoi glutei. Ma Nicholson si è solo illuso di aver inventato un nuovo tipo di sfrontatezza, perché nel gesto poco raffinato ha predecessori illustri: il principe Michele di Borbone Parma, compagno di Maria Pia di Savoia, che la settimana scorsa ha mostrato i glutei in segno di disprezzo per i fotografi. Non vorremmo fosse l'inizio di una nuova moda: dopo il seno delle donne, le rotondità maschili.

Boarding a tender en route to a friend's yacht in St. Tropez harbor, actor Jack Nicholson registered annoyance at the sight of the camera by turning his back and pulling down his pants. The sequence, which ran in the Italian Eva Express, was taken by Daniel Angeli and Jean-Paul Dousset, who spend summers on the Côte d'Azur looking for sensational photographs.

"Leave me in peace," cried pop singer Amanda Lear when photographer George Spitzer moved in for this close-up as she was emerging from a Paris clinic after an eight-day rest cure. Alerted to her departure, a flock of paparazzi descended upon the clinic at noon. But only Spitzer had the patience to outwait the singer and get this photograph late in the day; it accompanied a story about her recovery in Eva Express.

On a tip from an autograph hound, Ron Galella trailed Greta Garbo from a New York bookstore to the street where she lives. Galella jumped out of a doorway to snap this picture of the startled Garbo. Newsweek picked up the picture, a revealing study in the renowned actress' obsession with privacy.

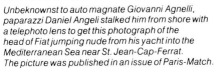

Unbeknownst to auto magnate Giovanni Agnelli, paparazzi Daniel Angeli stalked him from shore with a telephoto lens to get this photograph of the head of Fiat jumping nude from his yacht into the Mediterranean Sea near St. Jean-Cap-Ferrat. The picture was published in an issue of Paris-Match.

Perennial targets for paparazzi, Jacqueline Onassis and Frank Sinatra were caught by photographer Ron Galella leaving New York's 21 Club for the Rainbow Room. Galella tried to follow, but was chased off by a Sinatra bodyguard—an occupational hazard of paparazzi photography. The picture was used as a spoof on the month's news in National Lampoon, where it was captioned "Pic of the Month."

Shared Moments

Bed-and-bath pictures—pictures that seem to reveal unposed moments in celebrities' lives—are often the result of close collaboration between the photographer and his subjects. Together they may work out a scenario to project a desired image—domestic bliss, for instance. Or the celebrities may simply play themselves in everyday situations, with the camera looking on.

To illustrate a 1978 story on Betty Ford's courage in publicly acknowledging her problems with alcohol and drugs, Paris-Match turned to pictures by two photographers who had covered the First Family during Mrs. Ford's recovery from cancer surgery in 1974. The magazine used two pictures (right and top left) taken by David Kennerly, official White House photographer and Ford family friend. Darryl Heikes of UPI photographed the Fords kissing on the Truman balcony while attending a White House party.

En 1974, deja, elle avait provoqué l'admiration des Américains en reconnaissant que, atteinte d'un cancer, elle venait de subir l'ablation d'un sein.

Le toast de l'amour : mariés depuis 30 ans, les Ford envisagent le retour à la Maison Blanche : les prochaines présidentielles auront lieu dans deux ans.

Betty Ford, 60 ans, la femme de tous les courages est devenue une sorte d'héroïne nationale aux États-Unis. en déclarant publiquement : « Je prends trop de tranquillisants et trop d'alcool. Je ne peux pas continuer à lutter seule. Je rentre à l'hôpital où je vais subir un traitement de désintoxication ».

manière ouverte et audacieuse avec laquelle elle avoue coram publico autant ses convictions, ses craintes et sa résolution face à la maladie que son amour pour son époux. C'est ainsi que des millions d'Américains et téléspectateurs ont appris tour à tour que Betty allait subir l'ablation du sein, qu'elle était en faveur de l'avortement dans certains cas seulement et qu'elle aimait son mari comme par le passé. Au point, a-t-elle précisé, de connaître le bonheur conjugal très régulièrement.

Avant d'entrer à l'hôpital de Long Beach à Los Angeles, pour y subir sa cure de désintoxication, Betty Ford a eu ce mot émouvant : « J'aime la vie, j'aime les gens ». Puis, d'une voix où l'on discernait un peu de tristesse, elle a ajouté : « Je n'ai pas grand mérite à citer ainsi publiquement mes soucis personnels. Cela ne me pèse pas. Après trente ans de vie politique, je constate que notre vie entière, à Gerald et à moi, a été une vie publique ». ■

MAGDA PALACCI-BLEIER

Elle étonne les Américains par son irrésistible passion de la vérité: "J'entre en clinique parce que je bois"

Given only a few hours to photograph TV star John Ritter and his wife, Nancy Morgan, for a story in People, photographer Steve Schapiro sat down with the couple and "kicked around ideas" for projecting their marital bliss. The prankish Ritters made the assignment easy by coming up with lively picture suggestions, like sharing their bed with the family dog.

Dieter Klar's convincingly natural picture of German TV star Rudi Carrell bathing his year-old son Alexander came about because Klar, in a brief two days of shooting, was able to gain his subject's trust. Carrell, who agreed to a story on his home life for the German magazine Bunte, initially did not want Alexander to be a part of it. Klar persuaded him otherwise.

When Patrice Habans received exclusive rights to photograph Princess Caroline of Monaco and Philippe Junot during their Tahitian honeymoon, it was not only with the couple's active participation but with an apparent agreement that the newlyweds would share in the sale of the pictures. The Italian magazine Annabella reportedly paid Habans $10,000 for the pictures' first-time use.

Corporate Angels for Creative Projects

Big business joins government agencies and philanthropic foundations around the world to bankroll serious photographers

by Gene Thornton

Gene Thornton is the photography critic for *The New York Times* and a contributing editor of *ARTnews*. He is currently writing a history of photography.

The publication in 1978 of a sumptuous book, *Court House (page 47),* signaled the start of a new era in the long-standing relationship between business and photography. Suddenly, business has expanded its role; it is no longer just the client of commercial photography but now also is a patron of photographic art. Meanwhile, such traditional backers of serious photography as government agencies and charitable foundations have sharply increased their grants and fellowships.

The most dramatic change in the outlook for photographers is the availability of financing from large corporations. In the past, when business and industry gave money to photographers, they wanted photographs that helped them sell their products or polish their public image, and though they spent lots of money and often hired famous photographers, corporate need and not the photographer's vision was what counted. Today, although businesses still spend heavily for advertising and publicity photographs, a few corporations have also begun to support photographic projects that have nothing to do with the corporation's products or services, and that allow—indeed, encourage—the photographers to create the same kinds of photographs they would create on their own.

The best-known of these new projects is the $300,000 enterprise that culminated in the publication of *Court House.* Underwritten by Joseph E. Seagram & Sons, Inc., Canadian distillers who do a great deal of business in the United States, the Court House Project originated as a birthday present to the United States in its Bicentennial year. Twenty-four photographers (their average age was 30 in 1976) were given stipends, materials and travel expenses to photograph more than one third of the 3,043 county courthouses in the 48 contiguous states. Liquor bottles were to be kept out of the pictures—"It would be pretty tacky to get product involved in a project like this," says Seagram's board chairman Edgar Bronfman. Instead, the photographers were encouraged to bring their own vision to the project.

The resulting collection drew high praise. *The New York Times* compared it to the Farm Security Administration project of the 1930s, when a group of then mostly unknown photographers created an enduring portrait of America in the Great Depression. John Szarkowski, director of the Department of Photography at New York's Museum of Modern Art, gave the Court House Project an exhibition there.

Even more important, the Seagram's project encouraged another big corporation, the American Telephone and Telegraph Company, to follow suit. At first AT&T planned to hire well-known photographers to do the usual type of corporate-image project: a photographic essay on how the United States has been changed in the past 100 years by new forms of communication, particularly the telephone. But Renato Danese of the federal government's National Endowment for the Arts—who serves as a consultant to AT&T during his off-hours—persuaded the company to let the photographers photograph any aspect of American life that interested them. Says project director Max Schwartz, "We tried to pick outstanding photographers and then we left them alone, hoping they would create classic images."

For a pilot project, each of five photographers received $3,000 for his work and three sets of 15 prints, plus as much as $7,000 for expenses during a three-month assignment. In none of the pictures produced by the pilot project was there a telephone in sight, yet AT&T executives were so enthusiastic that they increased the number of photographers to 20, and have planned a series of traveling exhibitions beginning in 1979, and the publication of a book to be called *American Vision.*

In addition to commissioning new work, businesses have also begun to collect photographs and to support exhibitions at museums. In 1978 Springs Mills, Inc., a South Carolina textile manufacturer, agreed to finance a series of photography exhibitions at The Museum of Modern Art. "Photography has given us some of the most compelling images of our time," says Springs Mills president Peter G. Scotese. "It is an art that, in one way or another, touches virtually everyone."

Clearly other businessmen feel the same way. In recent years photography exhibitions have been underwritten by such corporations as Consolidated Edison of New York, Inc., and the Philip Morris Corporation, and by various manufacturers of cameras and film. Corporations have also begun to add photographs to their corporate art collections, and even to build collections consisting solely of photographs. The best-known corporate collection in the U.S. is probably that of The Exchange National Bank in Chicago. Initially selected under the guidance of historian Beaumont Newhall, it covers photography from the earliest days to recent years. The newest collection is the Target Collection of American Photography, now on a nationwide tour from its home base at the Museum of Fine Arts in Houston, Texas. A rapidly growing collection of 20th Century work, it is underwritten partly by Target Stores, Inc., of Texas, a division of the Dayton-Hudson Corporation.

The new interest in photography as art is not confined to business and industry. It is also felt by governments in many parts of the world and by the great foundations whose support of the arts has long been an important feature of American life. In recent years, support from these sources has greatly expanded and, in some cases, has taken new directions.

One of the first government-sponsored programs anywhere in the world intended to enable photographers to pursue artistic, rather than documentary, goals was the Photography Fellowship program of the National Endowment for the Arts, the agency of the federal government that is the principal source of noncommercial funds for the arts in the United States. In 1971, the first year of the NEA Photography Fellowship program, some 23 photographers were awarded fellowships averaging $2,000 each. For fiscal year 1979, 37 fellowships of $10,000 and 20 fellowships of $3,000 have been awarded. Photography underwritten by the NEA need not relate to any official policy except encouragement of the arts.

State governments are also financing art photography. The Massachusetts Arts and Humanities Foundation, now known as The Artist's Foundation, Inc., and New York state's Creative Artists Public Service program, better known as CAPS, offer grants similar to those of NEA. This kind of support for photography is also growing in several other countries. The Arts Council of Great Britain, the United Kingdom's equivalent of NEA, made its first major grant to an individual photographer in 1974, underwriting Ian Berry to document changes in English life. In that year 19 other photographers received smaller grants. By 1978 the Arts Council's major grant was £5,000 ($2,500), and two such grants were made. In Australia the Visual Arts Board of the Australia Council made its first grants to individual photographers in 1973. The Canada Council, which began its Photography Program in 1972, disbursed $240,000 in awards to photographers in 1977-78.

Even the venerable John Simon Guggenheim Memorial Foundation, long an important source of support for the arts in the United States, is taking a greater interest in photography. The foundation awarded its first fellowship to a photographer in 1937, when a grant of $2,500 enabled Edward Weston to spend a year photographing California and the West. During the next 30 years it awarded fellowships to more than 40 photographers. But it was not until the 1970s that the Guggenheim began to grant as many as 13 fellowships to photographers each year—a pace that shows no signs of letting up.

The expansion of this kind of support for photography is part of what is probably the most significant photographic trend of the past decade, the emergence of museums and galleries as primary showcases for new photographic work. Though photojournalism and magazine photography are far from dead *(pages 26-37),* they now compete with museums and galleries for the attention of the public. Museum and gallery photographers rarely make a living by the sale of their work, however, so the new noncommercial sources of funding are needed to keep them going.

Many older photographers who made their reputations as photojournalists in the 1930s, 1940s and 1950s are now subsidized by grants. Between 1956 and 1968 former *Life* photographer W. Eugene Smith, who died in October 1978 *(pages 228-233),* received not only NEA and CAPS grants but also three Guggenheim Fellowships. Similarly, the late John Vachon, a *Look* photographer for 23 years before that magazine folded in 1971, photographed small towns in the Midwest on a 1973 grant from the Guggenheim Foundation.

There is, in addition, a new generation of photographers whose work first reached the public through exhibitions and small-circulation books rather than through mass-circulation periodicals. Their careers would certainly have taken a very different turn, if indeed they had been possible at all, without the new sources of funds. This new generation of subsidized photographers was prominently featured in "Mirrors and Windows," The Museum of Modern Art's 1978 survey of American photography since 1960 *(pages 52-61).* Of the 101 photographers included in this show, most first came to public attention through exhibitions, and 75 had been awarded one or more of the major American grants. Four of the five photographers working on the AT&T pilot project have been Guggenheim Fellows.

It sometimes seems that the same handful of photographers receive most of the noncommercial support year after year, and that the same small group of people select them. Most grant-giving organizations try to change their panels of selectors

GRANTS FOR PHOTOGRAPHERS IN THE UNITED STATES

Source	Eligible Photographer
American Academy in Rome, Rome Prize Fellowship 41 East 65th Street New York, New York 10021	United States citizens
Apeiron Workshops, Inc. Peter Schlessinger Box 551 Millerton, New York 12546	United States citizens and residents
The Artists Foundation, Inc. 14 Beacon Street, Room 606 Boston, Massachusetts 02108	Residents of Massachusetts over 18 years of age
Bush Foundation E-900 First National Bank Building 332 Minnesota Street St. Paul, Minnesota 55101	Residents of Minnesota over 25 years of age
Creative Artists Public Service Program 250 West 57th Street New York, New York 10019	Residents of New York state
The John Simon Guggenheim Memorial Foundation 90 Park Avenue New York, New York 10016	Citizens and residents of the Western Hemisphere and the Philippines
Photographer's Fellowships Visual Arts Program National Endowment for the Arts Mail Stop 501 Washington, D.C. 20506	United States citizens and residents

Funds to underwrite individual American photographers in pursuing their creative work are available from the seven sources listed above. The number of grants available varies with the source. The most extensive support comes from the National Endowment for the Arts, which offers as many as 57 Photography Fellowships a year. In addition, grants of up to $20,000 occasionally are awarded to photographers by the Rockefeller Foundation in New York City and by the National Endowment for the Humanities in Washington, D.C.

Kind and Amount	Application Date
Lodging and studio space in Rome for one year, plus $4,800 stipend and up to $2,100 for travel and expenses	November 15
Lodging, meals, materials and darkroom space for four months at Apeiron Workshop	Interview by appointment
$3,500 for one year	March 15
Up to $12,000 for 18 months, plus up to $2,000 for travel and expenses	November 10
$3,500 to $5,000 for one year	Date unspecified as of January 1979
$10,000 to $12,000 for one year	October 1
$10,000 or $3,000 for one year	April 3

from year to year, but the pool of knowledgeable people from which they can draw is small, and the same names keep turning up. In addition to Renato Danese, assistant director of the NEA's Visual Arts Program, who helped to choose the photographers for the AT&T project, there is Szarkowski, who teamed with photographer Aaron Siskind to select the photographers for the Seagram's Court House Project. And though the NEA lays great stress on choosing panelists from different regions and with different points of view, still its list of consultants includes previous NEA award-winners as well as such ubiquitous curators and teachers as Peter Bunnell of Princeton University, Van Deren Coke of the University of New Mexico—and Szarkowski. In fact, Szarkowski, by virtue of his position at The Museum of Modern Art, is consulted by nearly everyone from the NEA to Seagram's, and though neither he nor the foundation will confirm or deny it, he is widely believed to be the *éminence grise* behind the Guggenheim's selections.

There are, however, literally hundreds of sources of noncommercial support for photographers besides the big foundations, corporations and government agencies. "Most young photographers," says Szarkowski, "think only of their own artistic goals and the big foundations that give them total freedom to pursue them. But there is almost always a business or government agency whose specific goals overlap with the photographer's goals and may even spur him on to do better work." Lida Moser, author of a book published in 1978, *Grants in Photography,* agrees. A New York-based photographer and writer, she, like Szarkowski, stresses the importance of looking for small, local sources of support that can be adapted to the photographer's own needs. She tells how a number of enterprising photographers of no particular fame found local support for their projects.

One such project that came to fruition in 1978 originated two years earlier when two Baltimore students and their instructor in a documentary-photography course began photographing the picturesque old neighborhoods of East Baltimore. The three women soon learned that East Baltimore was not only visually appealing but also an unusual example of an inner-city working-class area that has been preserved by its residents as a desirable place to live. Organizations and individuals that might not have been interested in three unknown photographers were interested in publicizing through photography this example of urban success; when the three photographers began to seek money to expand their activities, they found numerous sources of support, among them the NEA; the Baltimore Museum of Art; Baltimore City Hall, which provided space for an exhibition; and a local bakery, which helped cater the exhibition's opening reception.

This kind of local financing of photography is based on an appeal to the sponsor's interest in other than purely artistic aspects of photography. However, it has enabled many younger photographers to build their reputations so that they can compete successfully for support from corporations, government agencies and foundations, which now regard photography as an art that is the equivalent of painting, music and theater, and worthy of the same kind of support.

Fine Work from Grant Recipients

In 1978 the amount of money available worldwide to underwrite photography —and the total number of photographers receiving it—increased significantly. On the following pages are some examples of interesting or important international undertakings that have received funds from large corporations, private foundations and government agencies.

In a few cases, such as the mammoth Court House Project *(page 47),* the pictures are drawn from work begun two or three years ago and already completed. Most of the pictures, however, are from enterprises for which grant money is still being supplied.

The conditions under which the work is being done vary with each project and donor. Funding in some instances goes to a single photographer to do whatever he wants to do. In others, the project involves many photographers working within an established theme.

GEORGE KRAUSE: *From the series "I Nudi" (The Nudes),* 1977

U.S.A.—John Simon Guggenheim Memorial Foundation Fellowship, and Prix de Rome, American Academy in Rome

Krause's study of three nudes against a stucco wall was taken during his year's residency in Rome as recipient of two grants: the Prix de Rome, which includes the use of a studio in the American Academy in Rome as well as a stipend; and a Guggenheim. The Prix de Rome has no category for photography, so Krause applied in the field of environmental design. He is the first photographer to receive the award.

Australia—Australia Council
Visual Arts Board Special Project Grant

*Fascinated by the juxtaposition of housefront and
yard, Lojewski photographed this Art Deco façade with
appropriately stylized trees on a grant to document
the Australian environment. One of nine grants awarded
to photographers by the Board in 1976, it carried a
value of $1,500 for a project the Board regarded as short-
term. For ongoing projects the assistance offered
can be more than triple that amount.*

STEPHEN LOJEWSKI: *House in Sydney,* 1976

U.S.A.—National Endowment for the Humanities Summer Stipend

The regal Oba, or king, of a Yoruba town in Nigeria sat for Sprague during the photographer's 1975 project to study the way the Yoruba people have incorporated photography into their culture. The Oba's pose, repeated in the cutout photographs of him decorating the room, is traditional for ceremonial occasions.

STEPHEN SPRAGUE: *The King of Ila-Orangun,* 1975

U.S.A. — National Endowment for the Arts Survey Grant

To compare the America that was with the America that is, a team of photographers was granted funds to rephotograph sites visited by pioneer landscape photographers like Timothy O'Sullivan and William Henry Jackson on government-sponsored surveys of the American West between 1860 and 1890. The modern photographers, placing their cameras in the same locations as the 19th Century ones, got such dissimilar pairs of photographs as the two at right, where only part of the cliff face has remained the same, and such similar ones as the two below, in which only the names have changed in a century's time.

WILLIAM HENRY JACKSON: *Pulpit Rock, Utah,* 1869

THE REPHOTOGRAPHIC SURVEY PROJECT: *Location of Pulpit Rock, Utah,* 1978

WILLIAM HENRY JACKSON: *Whitehouse Mountain and Elk Lake, Colorado,* 1873

THE REPHOTOGRAPHIC SURVEY PROJECT: *Snowmass Mountain and Geneva Lake, Colorado,* 1977

U.S.A.—American Telephone & Telegraph Co. American Vision Project

A Colorado mountainside plunged into darkness by another mountain's shadow was photographed during a three-month pilot project subsidized by AT&T.

U.S.A.—Joseph E. Seagram & Sons Court House Project

A finely carved Victorian doorway in a Texas courthouse is one of Winningham's contributions to a Canadian distiller's bouquet to the U.S. in its Bicentennial year.

ROBERT ADAMS: *Arkansas River Canyon, Colorado, 1978*

GEOFF WINNINGHAM: *Hill County Court House,* 1976

SIGGEN STINESSEN: *London, 1977*

Norway—Norwegian Government Guaranteed Lifetime Income

Stinessen's poetic portrait of a young woman standing in the rain, gazing at her reflection in a mirror, is typical of the work that won him a state subsidy of $8,300 a year for the rest of his life. Stinessen, the first photographer to be given this award, was nominated for it by fellow Norwegian photographers.

The Major Shows/2

The Major Shows/2

Debuts in Latin America / LUIZ CARLOS FELIZARDO: *Cemetery at Santa Barbara do Sul, Brazil,* 1974

A Curator's Controversial Selection

Which was the "mirror," which the "window," was the game the audience played at John Szarkowski's categorization of two decades of American photography

Photographers, critics, curators and knowledgeable gallery-goers knew a major event was in the offing when John Szarkowski, influential director of the Department of Photography at The Museum of Modern Art in New York City, announced a plan to offer his own personal survey of American photography since 1960. But few suspected that the show, entitled "Mirrors and Windows," was going to be one of the museum's biggest attention-getters in recent memory. The exhibition, which will travel to eight major U.S. cities before the end of 1980, drew a quarter-million viewers during the two months it was on display in New York. Part of the reason for its popularity was that it brought together for the first time a large array of richly diverse pictures, and made it possible to see them as parts of an absorbing whole. But spicing the interest in the photographs was an outburst of critical comment of the sort usually reserved for visiting collections of exotic national treasures.

Part of the debate centered on Szarkowski's selections. Concentrating on the work of 101 contemporary photographers—Diane Arbus, Jerry Uelsmann, Lee Friedlander, Garry Winogrand and other established figures among them—the exhibition presented 189 images that ranged from snapshot-like portraits and television-dominated interiors to fragmented nudes and ambiguous dreamscapes with ghostly figures. All were pictures supporting Szarkowski's premise that the recent direction of photography "has been from public to private concerns." Notably absent, critics observed, was photojournalism, although the period covered by the show had produced many memorable images of war, riots and assassinations; only Irwin B. Klein's formally composed shot of a Minneapolis fire *(page 54)* looked at all like a news photograph.

Far sharper than the comment on selections was the critical discussion of the novel thesis around which Szarkowski organized the exhibit. As the name of the show indicates, the photographs were grouped into two categories: mirrors and windows. In Szarkowski's view, mirrors (shown on right-hand pages in the following portfolio) are intensely subjective photographs, with the photographer himself as the ultimate subject. Windows (on left-hand pages) look out on the world more objectively. A few pictures slipped easily into these molds. Linda Connor's ethereal nude self-portrait *(page 61)* is a classic example of photography's ability to dramatize autobiography. On the other hand, Garry Winogrand's photograph of two toddlers in a suburban driveway *(page 58)* shows the medium in a more documentary mode. But critics almost unanimously questioned whether the best of a highly creative period in American photography should be thus pigeonholed. Indeed, viewers visiting the exhibit were puzzled about which pictures fell into which group—no explanation was offered—until they deduced that mirrors were in silver-coated frames on gray walls, and windows in white frames on white walls.

BILL OWENS: *Ronald Reagan*, 1972

IRWIN B. KLEIN: *Minneapolis Fire*, 1962

ROBERT RAUSCHENBERG: *Kiesler*, 1966

MARIE COSINDAS: *Sailors*, Key West, 1966

PAUL CAPONIGRO: *Avebury Stone Circle*, Wiltshire, England, 1967

GARRY WINOGRAND: *Albuquerque, New Mexico,* 1957

ROGER MERTIN: *Tree in Rochester, New York*, 1973

KEN JOSEPHSON: *Stockholm Street Scene*, 1967

LINDA CONNOR: *Self-Portrait*, 1966

Making Fashion Come Alive

A traveling exhibition resurrects the half-forgotten works of Martin Munkacsi, the photojournalist who brought "a taste of honesty to a lying art"

"Never pose your subjects. Let them move about naturally. All great photographs today are snapshots. Don't let the pretty girl stop to put her hair to rights!" When Martin Munkacsi wrote those words in 1935, he was offering revolutionary advice to fashion photographers. An exhibition that was mounted last year, however, demonstrated just how well the Hungarian-born photojournalist-turned-fashion-photographer followed his own advice and determined the course fashion photography was to follow. The show, at New York City's International Center of Photography, presented more than 150 photographs spanning four decades; they lived up to the title, "Spontaneity and Style," for in Munkacsi's exuberant images the subjects more often than not are running, leaping or pursuing some other type of vigorous activity with total abandon.

Before Munkacsi arrived on the scene, nearly all fashion shots were made on elaborately furnished studio sets and recorded impeccably attired models frozen in stylish poses. In his work, mainly for the fashion magazine *Harper's Bazaar,* Munkacsi changed all that. He took swimsuits onto the beach, golf attire onto the links, streetwear into the streets, and whenever possible, he set models into motion. In the process, he did something even more important; he changed the image of the ideal woman from a pale, fragile creature into an active, alive person. "He brought a taste of happiness and honesty and a love of women," wrote Richard Avedon in homage to his predecessor as fashion's best-known photographer, "to what was, before him, a joyless, loveless, lying art."

More than anything else, what Munkacsi brought to fashion photography was the technique of the photojournalist. Born in 1896 in Hungary, Munkacsi at age 18 became a photographer for a Budapest newspaper. By 1927, he had parlayed an eye for action and a talent for self-promotion—"A picture isn't worth a thousand words; it's worth a thousand bucks," he once quipped—into a position as a globe-trotting photoreporter for Europe's largest weekly, *Berliner Illustrirte Zeitung* (Berlin Illustrated News). In 1934 the rise of Nazism led him to accept an offer from *Harper's Bazaar.* This transition from photojournalist to fashion photographer goes almost unnoticed in the exhibition. The photographs from the first half of his career merge almost imperceptibly with his later fashion work; on the page at right, only the title under the photograph hints to the viewer that the shot is a piece of shoreside reporting and not a picture of swimwear made on location. Munkacsi went on assignments loaded down with three or four large-format cameras, none smaller than $3^{1}/_{4}$ by $4^{1}/_{4}$ inches. But amazingly, he hand-held those clumsy instruments as easily and flexibly as if they were 35mm cameras to achieve the snapshot immediacy he sought.

Because Munkacsi worked for publication, he rarely kept original prints or negatives. Only years of research by Colin Osman, who organized the show with William Ewing, brought his zestful images back to life. As a result of their work, Munkacsi's legacy is now indisputable. "He did it first," wrote Avedon, "and today the world of what is called fashion is peopled with Munkacsi's babies, his heirs."

"Sweet Heinrich," the Candy Vendor on the Beach, c. 1930

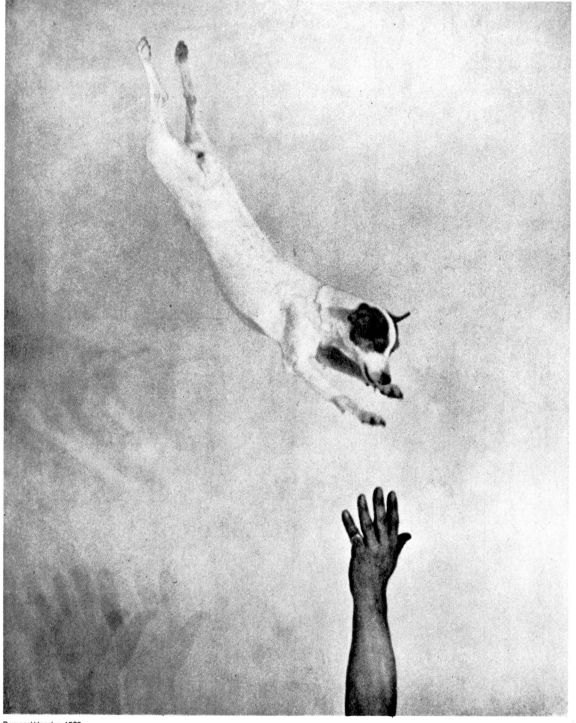

All that is known about this stop-action picture of a dog being tossed in the air is that it appeared in a German picture magazine, Die Woche (The Week), in the late 1920s or early 1930s. The show's curators reproduced it from a faded clipping that they found in one of the photographer's scrapbooks.

In this antic picture, which the photographer set up in a studio, a male dancer takes an acrobatic coffee break to the nonamazement of his seated companion. The picture originally appeared in the 1934 issue of a German photography annual, Das Deutsche Lichtbild (The German Photograph), which featured an introduction by Adolf Hitler.

Dog and Hand, c. 1929

Having Fun at Breakfast, 1934

Cruise Fashion, 1933

On his first assignment to shoot fashion photographs, Munkacsi broke with a tradition of studio posing by taking socialite-model Lucille Brokaw out to a Long Island beach and commanding her to run (left). "The resulting picture of a typical American girl in action, with her cape billowing out behind her, made photographic history," wrote Carmel Snow, editor of Harper's Bazaar, who commissioned the shot. By the time, only two years later, that Munkacsi used the same approach for a beach costume (right), he was at the top of his field.

Miami Fashion, 1935

Commissioned for a 1935 article on sunbathing, this beautifully composed picture of a supine nude beneath a semitransparent parasol was rejected by the editors of the magazine, who thought it too revealing. The exhibition's organizers discovered the unused negative among the photographer's files.

Sunbather, 1935

An assignment in the United States for a Berlin
magazine took Munkacsi to San Simeon, the California
estate of publisher William Randolph Hearst,
where he photographed Hearst's mistress, actress
Marion Davies, wearing an elaborately ruffled
organdy gown that contrasts with the terrace's stark
geometry. When Munkacsi later joined Hearst's
Harper's Bazaar, this picture ran as a fashion photograph.

Organza in Motion, 1934

Dancers in Flight, 1937

To illustrate a feature story on dance, Munkacsi staged this exuberant studio photograph of a visiting Japanese performer and his American partner.

In the striking picture at right, made for an article on exercises that promised to beautify the bosom, a model clad in a glittering skintight swimsuit performs a torso-twisting movement called the corkscrew.

The Corkscrew, 1937

Style in the Rain, 1934

A stylishly attired woman seems almost suspended from her parasol as she takes a flying leap across a rain-soaked curb. Like many of Munkacsi's pictures, this spectacular shot was used not to illustrate a particular new garment style but rather to set the tone for an article—in this case, one on spring rainwear.

"Pick unexpected angles," Munkacsi advised, "but never without reason." He followed his precept for pictures made at the 1939 World's Fair in New York City, combining imaginative placement of the model with an unusually low point of view that emphasizes the angularity of the Fair's stark, modern architecture.

Today against Tomorrow, 1938

Eye-opening Debuts in Latin America

Nearly 200 photographers little known in the States drew unprecedented numbers of viewers to Mexico City's Museum of Modern Art with pictures of great visual impact

Until recently, any mention of Latin American photography brought to mind colorful images of Indians and gauchos, or reportage of revolutions and earthquakes—more often than not the work of photographers from the United States or Europe. But the First Show of Contemporary Latin American Photography, an exhibition that opened in Mexico City in May 1978, consigned that notion to the past. Six hundred prints by 173 photographers representing 15 countries lined the walls of the National Museum of Modern Art. Ninety per cent of the photographers had never exhibited their work before. A crowd of 10,000—unprecedented for a photography show—thronged the museum each weekend while the pictures were on view.

The exhibition was part of a photographic festival that also included lectures, workshops and displays of 19th and early-20th Century photography at two other museums. The sponsor, the Mexican Council of Photography, expected difficulty in rounding up acceptable entries. In a vast region that includes 19 countries, there were no large photography associations or publications to spread the word; the organizers had to depend on an informal network of photographer-friends to nominate entries and solicit prints. When the council received 3,100 submissions, it was as much shocked as gratified.

According to Pedro Meyer, president of the council, many of the participants overcame formidable obstacles in order to enter their pictures. In Cuba, photographers were hampered by a shortage of enlarging paper; they gathered up the limited supply and divided it among themselves. In Brazil and Argentina, where mail is censored, participants could not be sure authorities would permit the shipment of such daring pictures as the Brazilian nude reproduced on page 78. "The photographers just put their pictures into the mail," said Meyer, "and prayed." Chile's repressive policies were not even challenged; no photographers living in Chile were invited. The only Chilean photograph represented in the exhibition came from a photographer in exile in Hungary.

The quality of the show in Mexico was worth the photographers' struggle. Among the pictures on display were surreal and abstract images that would have been at home in the avant-garde galleries of Europe or the United States. The majority of the photographs, however, could have been taken in no other part of the world—they were documentaries recording and commenting on the lives of Latin Americans. Nacho López, a member of the selection committee, expressed surprise at the number of photographs treating documentary themes. "Normally, we resent being thought of as a bloc or as a unit," he said, "so we make much of our regional differences and of our individuality, but when we look at the pictures we have been taking, we see a great deal that is the same."

Highlighted in the evening shadows, a receding line of plates set out for a holiday meal offers a striking study of perspective in the market plaza of a small town in Brazil. The photographer took this unusual shot at a local celebration known as the Feast of the Holy Spirit.

RICARDO NARDELLI MALTA: *Plates in a Courtyard*, São Luís do Paraitinga, Brazil, 1976

One of a series of portraits taken for a book about Latin American writers, this shot pictures Argentine author Ernesto Sabato apparently lost in thought on a bench in a leaf-strewn park. The photographer—one of Argentina's best-known—chose the setting because the park figures significantly in a Sabato novel.

In a small village on the Atlantic coast of Panama, Josepha, an herbal healer and priestess of a local cult, performs a rite intended to protect a child from the influence of the evil eye. The photographer spent three years preparing a book in the remote community, which was founded by runaway slaves. During some of that time she stayed with Josepha, whom she characterizes as the backbone of the village.

SARA FACIO: *Ernesto Sabato in Lezama Park*, Buenos Aires, 1969

SANDRA ELETA: *Josepha Curing a Child of the Evil Eye*, Portobelo, Panama, 1976

A jacketed nude stands with defiantly casual openness in front of a remote Brazilian chapel, its façade suggesting a face agape. As striking in subject matter as it is exaggerated in contrast and graininess, the picture is from a series on two young sisters, Anna and Adriana, that has been in preparation for more than four years.

ODILÓN DE ARAUJO: *Adriana*, Lagoa Santa, Brazil, 1977

Posed with his conga drum, to which he has tacked a strange pair of eyes, a cigar-smoking musician named Pedro stands outside a metalsmith's shed —a Sunday meeting place for former members of conga bands. This exuberant image of Pedro was shot for a book on Havana's fraternity of retired musicians.

MARÍA E. HAYA (MARUCHA): *Pedro*, Havana, 1970

Mexican photographer Pedro Meyer set this scene,
intentionally making a picture that is both a sympathetic
portrait of his mother attended by her servants, and
an indictment of a life style he considers exploitive. "By
photographing the wealthy," Meyer explains,
"I end up making a statement about the poor, with all its
social and political implications."

PEDRO MEYER: *A Sunday at My Mother's House*, Mexico City, 1977

The shadowy shapes of a woman and her companion leaving an apartment building combine with the angular lines of carpet and door fittings to create a diagonal composition centered on the woman's leg. In such fragmentary urban scenes, d'Ávila tries to contrast the linear forms of architecture with the natural curves of the human body.

ANTONIO CARLOS S. D'ÁVILA: *Untitled*, São Paulo, Brazil, 1977

On a visit to the picturesque old town of Colonia, which
faces Buenos Aires across the Río de la Plata,
Argentine photographer Sara Facio took this picture
of Uruguayan children crowding a window of an
old house to watch passing tourists. In 1965 the picture
became the first photograph to be reproduced
on an Argentine postage stamp.

SARA FACIO: *Looking at Life*, Colonia, Uruguay, 1963

In a small colonial plaza in Old Havana dominated by a two-story cutout of Fidel Castro, a man pedals two children home from school. This image, with its abrupt contrasts in size and in the spirit of past and present, was the handiwork of a 22-year-old magazine reporter on an assignment to shoot street preparations for a Communist Party congress.

ROGELIO LÓPEZ MARIN (GORI): *On the Streets of Havana, Cuba*, 1975

Heritage of the Concerned Thirties

The social commentary of the Photo League, which used New York City streets as a studio, is given renewed relevance in a display touring the United States and Canada

In 1938 a mimeographed newsletter mailed to museums and galleries proclaimed: "Photography has tremendous social value. Upon the photographer rests the responsibility and duty of recording a true image of the world as it is today." This manifesto summarized the purpose of a unique experiment in photography—the Photo League, a group of reform-minded photographers in New York City who left an indelible mark on the making of documentary images. In 1978, for the first time since the League closed its doors more than a quarter of a century ago, the works of 67 of its members, staff and advisers were brought together in "Photographic Crossroads: The Photo League," a show staged first in Ottawa at the National Gallery of Canada in April, and later in New York, Houston and Minneapolis.

The League was organized in 1936, a product of the often-radical social consciousness of the Depression. It aimed to arouse public concern for the poor and downtrodden with skillfully rendered documentary photographs, emulating Lewis Hine's earlier shots of working children, Eugène Atget's Parisian street scenes and Farm Security Administration photographers' images of rural poverty. "The streets of New York are the League's most important studios," the newsletter declared, and the members, mostly young and many themselves products of the city's tenements, undertook a remarkable series of group projects. They recorded life among Harlem's blacks, the Bowery's derelicts, the Lower East Side's Jews, the Chelsea district's Irish and, as counterpoint, among Park Avenue's affluent.

At the time, no similar group existed, and its headquarters—in a series of meagerly furnished lofts and basements—became a major photographic center. Noted photographers—Paul Strand, Berenice Abbott and Margaret Bourke-White among them—acted as advisers. Others, such as Edward Weston, Robert Capa, Roy Stryker and Henri Cartier-Bresson, exhibited their works and spoke at the League. This mixture of successful elite and impoverished beginners sometimes went sour. Once, a member says, "Ansel Adams lectured to kids with holes in their pockets about gold-toning their prints." But for young photographers seeking serious training, the League offered inexpensive courses; exacting, inspiring instructors such as Sid Grossman; and communal darkrooms where chemicals cost a dime. To many, it was a second home. "There was," a former student recalls, "that smell of creativity, staying up till 4 a.m., smoking and talking about photographs."

Because of the often-leftward—sometimes outright Communist—leanings of the League's leaders, it fell victim to the Cold War. In 1947, the Attorney General listed it as an organization believed to be subversive to the U.S., in effect blacklisting members so that they had difficulty getting work. Many friends of the League, outraged by this seemingly unjustified interference, came to the members' defense, and at first the group rebounded from the blow. As East-West tensions deepened, however, that support slowly dissolved, and in 1951 the Photo League went out of existence. But its legacy was a generation of documentary photographers trained to combine personal insight with craftsmanship. As the exhibit makes clear, that combination produced not only a true image of the world but an enduring one.

At St. Joseph's House, a home for indigent men and women in New York's Little Italy, one resident sits idly in the barren backyard while another, silhouetted in the passageway, watches passersby in the street. Taken by Aaron Siskind, who directed most of the League's projects, this picture was part of a study on the Catholic Worker Movement—a group that led a communal life according to primitive Christian principles. The picture's title is a Biblical quotation from a lament by Christ on homelessness.

AARON SISKIND: *Foxes Have Holes*, 1939-40

CLEMENS KALISCHER: *Displaced Persons*, New York City, 1948

The drab scene below, of a clothesline-draped slum dwelling, was photographed by a onetime League president for a book about Los Angeles.

MAX YAVNO: *Los Angeles Tenement,* 1949

TED TESSLER: *Chelsea*, New York City, 1950

Part of a series about life in a tenement district of Manhattan, this picture of a little girl waiting for her father outside a bar was taken by a photographer who joined the League during its waning years. After the group was dissolved, Tessler recalls, he was one of several members who continued to meet regularly on Fridays for sessions at which "analysis of a single photograph occasionally lasted until dawn."

Against an arched opening in a railway viaduct, men play ball and an awkwardly poised little girl reaches for her bottle-cap marker in a game of hopscotch. The picture is from a series on New York's East Harlem. The photographer, a leader in the League, spent a year on the project, which like many of the group's documentaries focused on one street so that the photographers could better understand the residents.

WALTER ROSENBLUM: *Hopscotch—East 105th Street*, New York City, 1950

GLORIA NARDIN WATTS: *Bobby Vinci*, Queens, New York, c. 1950

The turn away from social involvement during the early postwar years is evident in this portrait of an introspective teenager—the photographer's brother—leaning on a kitchen doorjamb. The picture was shown in one of the last exhibits sponsored by the Photo League.

Only a mild curiosity at the presence of the camera encroaches on the impassive expressions of a woman and a boy at New York City's most famous beach. The photographer, just 17 years old at the time, was a beginning student at the League. "Photo League was very important in that search for yourself," he now says. "I never thought of having my pictures exhibited; they were important in terms of me."

SIDNEY KERNER: *Coney Island*, 1937

In a telling scene of life in Southern slums, a pregnant teenager sits on a bed in a room that is devoid of decoration except for a tattered soft-drink advertisement. The photographer, a League president who before his death in 1973 became one of Life magazine's best-known staffers, once said: "I can't look at a tenement without wanting to tear it down."

By canting this shot taken in midtown Manhattan, the photographer emphasized the checkerboard-like pattern created by movie billboards and two newly constructed skyscrapers with a Gothic school building between them. Although Steiner, an established film maker, was an instructor at the League, he frequently disagreed with its leaders' leftist political philosophies, and was more interested in creating artistic photographs than in promoting social reform.

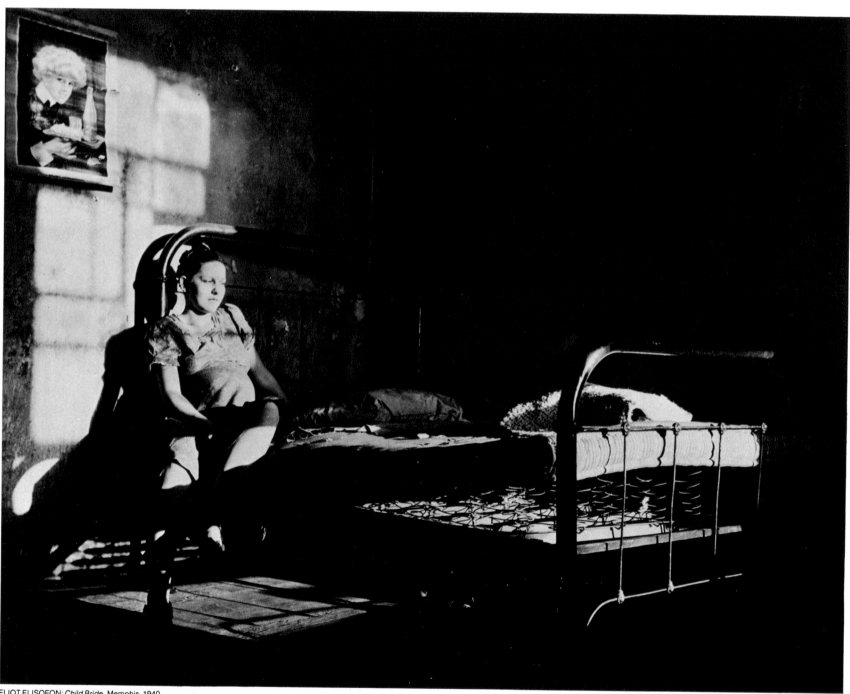

ELIOT ELISOFON: *Child Bride*, Memphis, 1940

RALPH STEINER: *Lexington Avenue at 51st Street*, New York City, 1932

*An interplay of circles is captured in this picture,
the rings on the dress of a passing woman repeating a
similar pattern of glass disks embedded in the
pavement. The photographer says that many of his
fellow League members dismissed his work
as frivolous because he was more concerned with "how
people looked next to buildings, walls, sidewalks"
than with revealing their social condition.*

RUDY BURCKHARDT: *New York City*, 1939

Part of a series on a lower Manhattan block, this freeze-action shot of a girl soaring on a swing under the looming silhouette of a bridge was one of the first pictures ever taken by the photographer, now a noted professional. Like many other League members, he started by recording familiar terrain. "I grew up on the Lower East Side," he says. "If I took pictures on Pitt Street, that's because that is where my heart lay."

WALTER ROSENBLUM: *Girl on a Swing near the Williamsburg Bridge,* New York City, 1939

SID GROSSMAN: *Henry Modgilin*, Oklahoma, 1940

A gaunt Oklahoma farmer gestures in front
of his shack as he talks to the photographer.
Grossman, who died in 1955, was the
most famous of the League's instructors.

In the lobby of a government building in downtown San Juan, a boy on crutches and a wizened old woman wait to go upstairs for assistance. The photographer, after receiving his early training at the League, became well known as a maker of documentary films.

LOU STOUMEN: *Woman with Crippled Boy*, San Juan, Puerto Rico, 1942

The Major Shows

Choices from a Feast of Images

In 1978 a record number of must-see exhibitions—from 130-year-old daguerreotypes and avant-garde color to multimedia prints—delighted the public

In 1978, museums and galleries around the world displayed the diverse work of photographers, both known and unknown, in unprecedented numbers. Among the highlights in this feast of images were experimental color work in London, Montreal and Rochester, New York, intriguing photocollages in Rhode Island and Iran, and historic pictures in Paris and Washington, D.C. One retrospective examined the entire career of a famous photographer. There were many shows worthy of attention; the following pages show one picture each from 10 of the most interesting.

The cornucopia of shows in 1978 was a natural outcome of the now-universal recognition of photography as an art form. "The general public," says Charles Traub, director of New York City's prestigious Light Gallery, "is becoming more and more aware of photography as *the* medium of contemporary art." When the Light Gallery opened just seven years ago, it was one of a handful of commercial galleries devoted to photographic prints, and one of only a few dozen places that gave any wall space at all to photographs. Today, in New York City alone, prints are regularly exhibited in more than 20 galleries as well as in eight museums, and in some 13 smaller showplaces that are operated primarily by colleges and similar institutions.

Across the United States and also in Europe, photographic displays are blossoming with equal vigor. In Washington, D.C., there were more than 50 notable exhibitions in 1978, including the first photographic show ever originated by the National Portrait Gallery *(page 103)*. The Nexus Gallery in Atlanta, which in 1973 could attract only the friends of its member-photographers to its openings, now draws crowds of 300 to 500 people. In Paris, a separate photography department under its own director is part of the new Georges Pompidou Center, the huge and controversial national art complex. Nearby, the Zabriskie Gallery of New York opened a Paris branch to deal exclusively in photographs.

For those who enjoy fine pictures, the multiplicity of shows finally brought the opportunity, long available in the other arts, to examine not only the current work of established artists but also to discover rising stars. And for photographers, the shows meant a new kind of fulfillment—the chance not only to find recognition for their own work but to see what their fellows were doing.

Foundry Gallery — Washington, D.C.

*The gables of a hedge-obscured house, strong elements
in themselves, are dramatically heightened by
infrared film, which darkens the sky, lightens the clouds
and intensifies the texture of the roof and vegetation.
Such moody infrared landscapes by this photographer
were shown in 1978 not only at a one-man show at the
Foundry Gallery but also at the University of Delaware
and at the Phot-Univers at Bièvres, near Paris.*

TOM SHULER: *Newark, Delaware,* 1977

99

Camerawork Gallery—San Francisco

*A cityscape shot from the top of the state capitol in
St. Paul, Minnesota, contrasts a gridwork of streets with
an unexpected close-up of the building's equestrian
statue. A concern with shapes and tones characterized
the work of the majority of the 21 contributors to
a show by contemporary California photographers.*

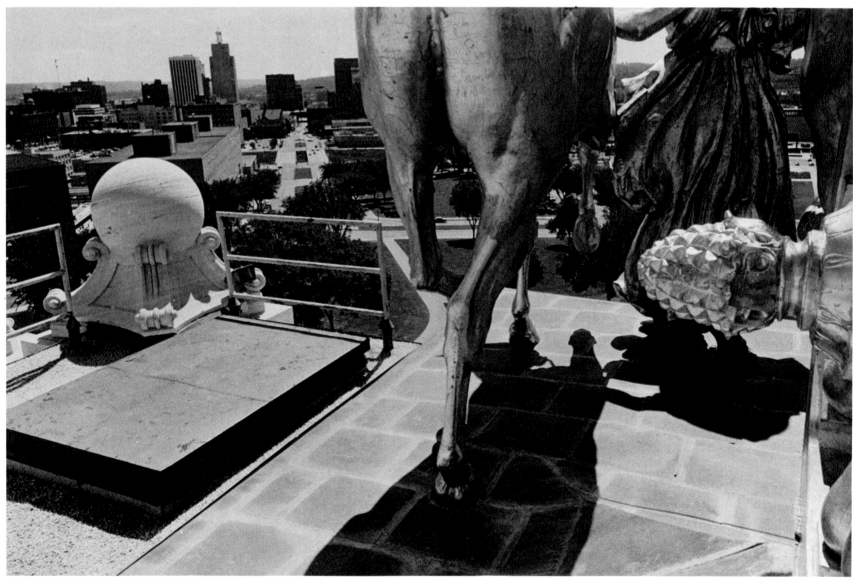

TIMO PAJUNEN: *St. Paul, Minnesota,* 1977

The Photographers' Gallery
—London

Looking like a detail from a fading fresco, this image of a nude in the classic stance of an urn-bearing maiden is based on a painting by the 19th Century French artist Ingres. It was created by placing a reproduction of the painting in contact with Polaroid Type 55 film, which yields both a negative and print in black and white. During exposure, the film was immersed in dye for coloration, producing what Cordier calls a photo-chemigram.

PIERRE CORDIER: *Photo-chemigram after "La Source" by Ingres,* 1978

Rochester Institute of Technology
—Rochester, New York

A mystifying photograph of a trash can and bent tubing against a slatted fence was created by moving the camera to blur the background, while using a flash to freeze the foreground. The tubing appears to be broken because, between the slats, the light-colored metal blends with the smeared sky.

MARK KLETT: *Breckenridge, Colorado, 1977*

National Portrait Gallery
—Washington, D.C.

A portrait of Emily Dickinson as a young student at Mount Holyoke College is the only photograph ever taken of the secretive 19th Century poet. One of 110 daguerreotypes of prominent Americans in a show at the National Portrait Gallery, the picture was taken by an unknown itinerant photographer who stayed at the school briefly. The headmistress dismissed him, fearing he distracted her young ladies from their studies.

PHOTOGRAPHER UNKNOWN: *Emily Dickinson at Seventeen,* c. 1847

Société Française de Photographie—Paris

In this late-1930s tableau of Soviet farm workers celebrating harvest's end, the workers are dusted by a wheat-threshing machine while a brass band, just a few yards away, remains distinct. The picture was one of 39 selected for an exhibition of Russian prints.

SERGEI CHIMANSKI: *The Last Day of Wheat Threshing*, late 1930s

Light Gallery—New York City

Straightforward, sharply detailed and carefully printed, this image of two tiny figures playing tennis on an isolated court in the lengthening shadows of evening is suffused with a pastoral calm. Like the majority of Gohlke's work during the last 11 years, nearly all of the 45 photographs that made up this one-man exhibit are tranquil, poetic landscapes discovered in the midst of the modern bustle of Minnesota's Twin Cities.

FRANK GOHLKE: *Tennis Court on the Outskirts of St. Paul, 1977*

Rhode Island School of Design
—Providence

*In a mixture of media, John Wood arranged a pair
of photographs and a copying-machine print against a
segment of one of his own drawings, then made
this negative print of the result. Wood, a professor of
design at Alfred University in Alfred, New York,
was one of the seven innovators in the Rhode Island show.*

JOHN WOOD: *Negative Print of a Collage,* 1977

Optica, a Centre for Contemporary Art—Montreal

Taken on the walkway of a viaduct in Rochester, New York, this geometric composition plays a subtle trick on the viewer by linking the colors of a distant smokestack with colored horizontal barrier pipes in the foreground, making the two extensions of each other. Such lively visual puzzles are a specialty of Bishop, a 32-year-old photography instructor.

MICHAEL BISHOP: *Rochester, New York,* 1978

University of Tehran—Iran

*Against a shot of a richly mosaicked mosque interior,
a collage was assembled from photographic cutouts of a
young girl, snakes and two wood screws. Then the
result was rephotographed on instant film. In addition to
experimental work, the one-man show included the
photographer's documentary coverage of life in Iran.*

KAVEH GOLESTAN: *From the series "Of Beasts and the Wild,"* 1977

The Annual Awards/3

The Annual Awards/3

DAVID ALAN HARVEY: *Woman in the Rain,* 1976

Magazine Photographer
of the Year—U.S.A.

*Like a translucent curtain, a sudden monsoon rain falls
across the mouth of a conduit sheltering a Malaysian
woman. The award was one of several presented under
the auspices of the University of Missouri.*

A World Transformed by Camera Magic

Imaginative picturetaking and printing techniques added extra drama to pictures winning this year's awards

Technical trickery marked a surprising number of the pictures honored with international awards during 1978. Several of the winning photographers exploited in unusual ways the capacities of lenses and cameras, while others achieved startling effects with "wrong" exposures or processing techniques, or by employing special attachments for their enlargers. And yet traditional techniques were not overlooked; in many of the prize photographs, strong composition lifts rather ordinary subjects to the level of lasting art.

The picture on pages 124-125 of a delivery truck stopping along the French countryside is given a new twist by a photographer who developed his color negative film as if it were a slide, producing a grainy, softly hued print that has the slightly blurred, atmospheric look of an Impressionist painting. The sensuously twining nudes on page 116 are another product of darkroom magic. The negative of a nude was placed in an enlarger whose lens was fitted with a partially opaqued mirror. The device split the projected image in two, resulting in a print that contained the original nude and her darker mirror image.

Light used in a more dazzling way helped photographers win two other major awards. The British award for Sports Photographer of the Year went to a man whose sparkling picture of a horse race *(page 114)* was made by moving a zoom lens as the horses drove toward the wire; the result imparts a feeling of explosive motion. To transform an otherwise routine picture of recruits in boot camp, an American photographer deliberately underexposed his film to accentuate shadows and the light-etched profiles of the young sailors *(page 115)*.

In contrast to these artifices were prize pictures that relied on basic principles. Framing doll-like houses on a Japanese hillside with a trellis *(opposite)* produced an austerely beautiful study. Another prizewinner *(page 126)* used careful composition to turn a veiled Indian bride into a stylized figure who seems to symbolize a still-mysterious India. This picture received one of three awards that went to photographs from *National Geographic,* which also published the unusual view of a monsoon on the preceding page and the majestic onion-domed cathedral in the Soviet Union on page 123.

In the hands of creative photographers, even such frequently photographed subjects as war and crime take on unusual qualities of compassion and power. A Vietnamese refugee using a towel to shield her child from the sun *(page 118)* looks like an Oriental madonna. And blacks fleeing tear gas thrown at them by South African policemen stampede toward the camera in a long, twining line that almost seems choreographed *(page 119)*. Pulitzer Prizes went to two photographers whose work is marked by a grim formality. The picture on page 130 of a white officer brandishing a pistol at a neat line of black civilians is one of several views of guerrilla war in Rhodesia that won the feature photography award. The spot-news Pulitzer Prize was awarded for the frightening picture on page 128 of a hostage being held with a shotgun wired around his neck—but in an unusual gaffe, the award initially went to the wrong photographer because of a mix-up in negatives.

Nendo Sho (Annual Award)—Japan

*Tiny houses on a misty hillside seem to be sheltered
beneath the strong diagonal of a leafy trellis.
The picture, reminiscent of a 19th Century Japanese
print, is part of a book on Minami's village that earned the
photographer an Annual Award, one of three given
this year by the Japan Photographic Society.*

YOSHIKAZU MINAMI: *View of Chichibu,* 1977

Sports Photographer
of the Year—Great Britain

Horses and jockeys seem to explode at the viewer in this shot taken from the spectators' gallery behind the finish wire at England's Goodwood racetrack. As the horses thundered toward the photographer, he pressed the shutter and shifted the zoom lens on his camera from 400mm to 200mm. The horse in the middle, somewhat more sharply focused than the others, is from Queen Elizabeth's stable.

GERRY CRANHAM: *Horse Race,* 1977

Newspaper Photographer
of the Year—U.S.A.

To make these men at Illinois's Great Lakes Naval Training Center appear outlined in light, Wirtz underexposed so that detail disappears and only the highlights stand out in the window-lit room. He won the award, administered by the University of Missouri, for handling "a variety of subjects with compassion."

MICHAEL WIRTZ: *Parade Rest*, 1977

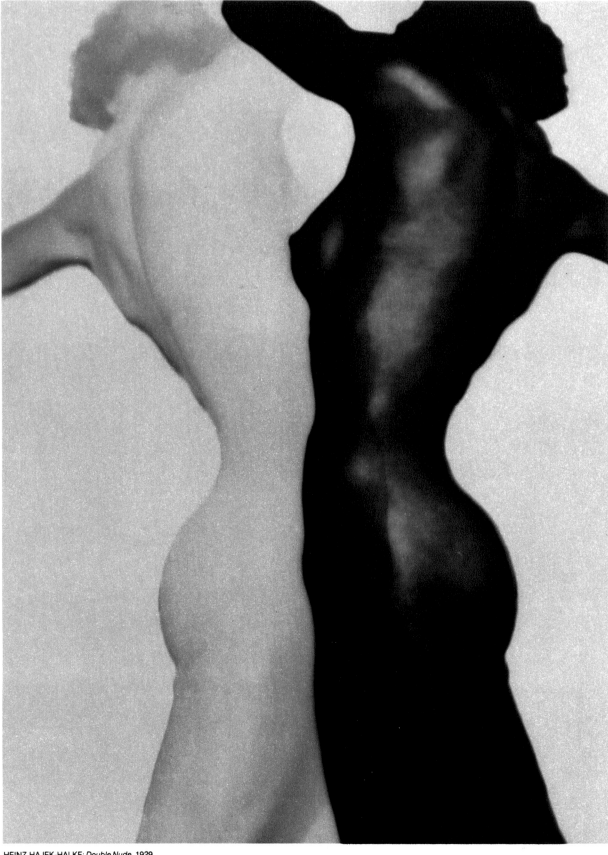

David Octavius Hill Medal —Germany

The Society of German Photographers' award was presented for a lifetime's work by two octogenarians of greatly different style. One award went to Hajek-Halke, who made these nude images in 1929 by placing a semiopaque mirror at a 45° angle between enlarger lens and paper. In contrast is the straightforward photograph by Moegle, in which the interplay of structural forms, light and shadow, rather than darkroom alteration, produces a powerful composition.

HEINZ HAJEK-HALKE: *Double Nude*, 1929

WILLI MOEGLE: *House Entrance*, 1940

EDDIE ADAMS: *Vietnamese "Boat of No Smiles,"* 1977

Robert Capa Gold Medal—U.S.A.

The plight of thousands of Vietnamese refugees is captured in the face of this peasant woman who, waiting stoically among coils of rope in a small boat, attempts to shield her son from the heat. The photographer was honored for this photograph and others in a portfolio on Vietnamese refugees.

Press Photo of the Year Award
—The Netherlands

*Black South Africans protesting the demolition
of their homes in Modderdam, a squatters' camp near
Cape Town, seem to perform a serpentine dance
as they flee tear gas thrown at them by policemen.*

LESLIE HAMMOND: *Tear Gas Terror*, 1977

Le Prix Nadar—France

A disquieting sense of menace is projected by this vignette of a small boy running between shadowed adults in a squalid gypsy village in eastern Czechoslovakia. Koudelka, himself Czech, won the Prix Nadar for his mysterious, sometimes frightening, images of life in the ghettos these gypsies call home. The photographs were taken some years ago, but Koudelka's book, "Gypsies," was not published until 1975, and this award for it was presented in 1978.

JOSEF KOUDELKA: *Gypsies,* 1966

**Shinjin Sho
(Newcomer Award)—Japan**

*Gocho was cited by the Japan Photographic Society
for his book of portraits, "Self and Others," which
includes this study of Japanese boys in a light-
dappled, bucolic corner of a crowded land. The prize
was one of three that were presented by the society
to young Japanese photographers.*

SHIGEO GOCHO: *Two Boys,* 1973

World Understanding Award—U.S.A.

Topped with golden Orthodox crosses, the star-studded onion domes of the Cathedral of the Nativity of the Virgin in Suzdal, a medieval town 120 miles northeast of Moscow, almost overwhelm a troop of nursery-school children frolicking below. Conger was honored for a photographic odyssey that took him from Soviet deserts to the far reaches of Siberia.

DEAN CONGER: *Cathedral of the Nativity of the Virgin,* Suzdal, U.S.S.R., 1975

ALAIN CHARTIER: *Country Scene,* 1977

Le Prix Niepce—France

What might otherwise have been a prosaic scene—a delivery truck stopping by a country house in Nery—is suffused with muted, hazy light by a special developing process: a color negative was developed by the method normally used for transparency film. Enlarged, the result was this amber-toned, grainy print, one of a group of Picardy scenes that earned Chartier the award given each year to promising newcomers.

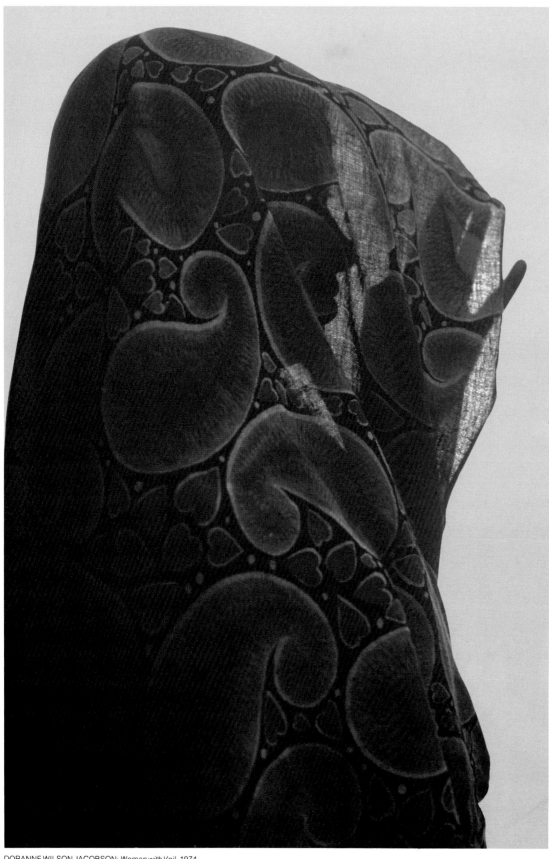

DORANNE WILSON JACOBSON: *Woman with Veil*, 1974

Dr. Erich Salomon Prize
—Germany

As stylized as a statue, a young Indian bride withdraws beneath the boldly patterned veil that custom requires her to wear in the presence of older villagers. This is one of the pictures that helped win National Geographic magazine the Salomon Prize, which is given by the German Photographic Society to honor a periodical's "exemplary use of photography in journalism."

Best Press Contributions
of the Year—U.S.S.R.

The top award of the Soviet Journalists' Union was presented to two photographers, Sergei Smirnov and Alexander Steshanov, who worked as partners photographing their native cities of Leningrad and Moscow. This view of Leningrad's Palace Square—photographed from a helicopter to stress the symmetrical façade of the Winter Palace, while giving the square itself the appearance of an enormous chessboard—was among those by Smirnov.

SERGEI SMIRNOV: *Palace Square*, 1977

*As police watch helplessly, Anthony Kiritsis holds
a sawed-off shotgun wired to the neck of Richard Hall, an
executive of a firm Kiritsis accused of swindling him.
The announcement awarding the Pulitzer Prize for this
picture got almost as much attention as the event it
recorded. Initially the award went to the wrong person.
Several photographers had been on the scene, and
not until the Pulitzer committee compared negatives did
it realize that the award should have been Blair's.*

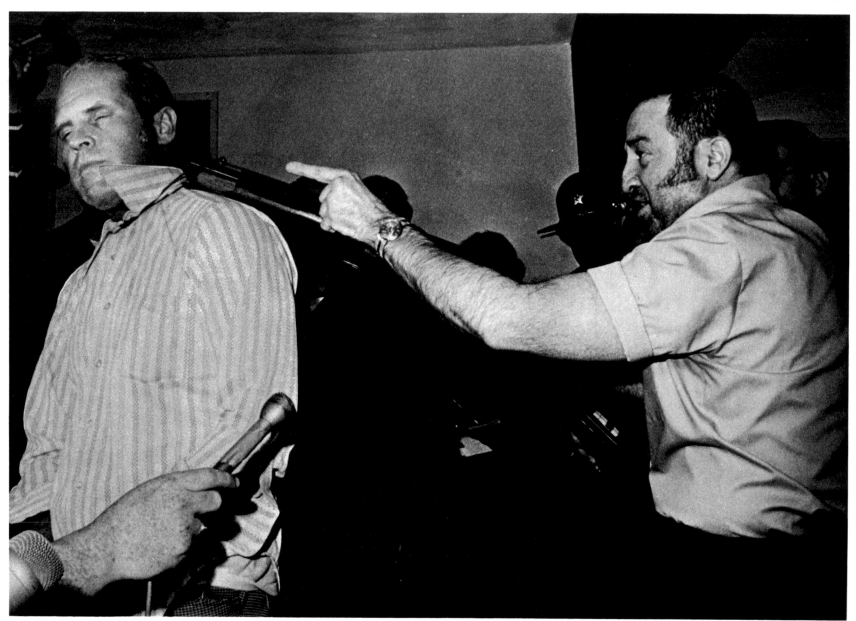

JOHN W. BLAIR: *Moment of Truth*, 1977

Kulturpreis—Germany

For a lifetime spent recording the intimate lives of such writers and artists as Colette, Virginia Woolf, Henri Matisse and James Joyce—shown here relaxing in a Paris garden with his son's family—Freund received the Kulturpreis, awarded by the German Photographic Society for outstanding achievement in photography.

GISELE FREUND: *James Joyce and Family*, 1938

**Pulitzer Prize for
Feature Photography—U.S.A.**

*Wielding a cocked pistol, a Rhodesian soldier
forces villagers to lean on their fingers and toes in the
hot afternoon sun. Baughman got this picture and others
showing maltreatment of black civilians during two
weeks he spent accompanying an elite antiguerrilla unit
in the field. Baughman was criticized for donning a
Rhodesian army uniform to facilitate his coverage.*

J. ROSS BAUGHMAN: *Interrogation,* 1977

The New Technology/4

The New Technology/4

Using an optical instrument called an interferometer, a technician checks the wavy curvature of the new plastic aspherical lens elements from the Kodak Ektramax 110 camera (pages 144-147). The lens, centered in a circular three-pronged bracket at lower right, glows red from the light of a laser beam that hits it. The reflected beam interacts with another reflected by a mirror to create a striped "interference pattern" of light on the interferometer screen. If the stripes are parallel and close together, the lens curvature is correct.

Dawn of an Era / NEIL MONTANUS: *Test Pattern for a Lens*

Dawn of an Era: Fast, Electronic, Computerized

Space-age science brings advances in lenses, film and automated controls that make the camera a true extension of the human eye

The year 1978 was a watershed in the technology of photography. Hopes nursed by generations of photographers for convenience, versatility and practicality were finally realized. In lenses *(pages 144-147)*, cameras *(pages 136-143)* and films *(pages 148-152)*, new developments heralded significant changes in the way pictures could be made and set the shape of photography for a generation to come.

The three aspects of photographic technology that most directly affect the making of pictures—speed, automation and camera design—were altered in 1978. Fast lenses and film, able to take good pictures unassisted by flash in dim light, finally became available inexpensively; together they make it practical to photograph wherever the eye can see. Automatic focusing gained wider use. And equally significant, automatic exposure became more sophisticated, adjustable for control manually or automatically. Fundamental to this elaborate automation was a transformation of the works inside the camera from a maze of gears, springs and levers to electronic chips forming computerized circuits; the newest cameras are directed by quite intelligent brains of their own, which keep the human operator informed of what they are doing through panels of flashing lights.

Among these major aspects of picturemaking, the one that may have the greatest impact on creative freedom is speed. It depends on both lens and film: a fast lens can make up for slow film and, conversely, fast film can make up for a slow lens. In 1978 both jumped upward in speed. New combinations of shutter speeds and f-stops broadened the photographer's palette. Faster shutter speeds could be used to stop action, smaller apertures to increase depth of field. And it became possible to develop a color documentary photography to complement the black-and-white documentaries of the past—especially in the artificially lit night world.

The gain in lenses came from perfection of an economical method for making lens elements that are aspherical, having a slightly uneven curvature instead of an arc uniformly spherical. The new aspherical elements are plastic, popped in quantity out of molding machines instead of being ground from glass laboriously and expensively. Plastic aspherics make possible a very sharp, fast lens with fewer elements—even snapshot cameras can now have quality lenses of f/1.9 or f/2 rating, comparable to standard professional equipment. And for professionals, aspherical lenses bring a broader promise; because they reduce the number of elements required in any kind of lens, they presage great improvements in specialty lenses such as zoom lenses that ordinarily require many elements.

Even an f/1.9 lens is not fast enough for most shooting in ordinary light indoors unless it is coupled with high-speed, fine-grained film—an ASA rating of 400 and a diaphragm setting of f/1.9 permit a 1/30-second exposure under those conditions. This rating was reached for black-and-white films in 1960, for color-print film in 1976, but not until 1978 for color-slide film. Finally, the photographer has available a full range of film types that combine high speed with grain fine enough for detail in the enlargements required by the tiny images on 110 and 135 (35mm) films.

This new combination of lenses and film makes it possible for any photographer to make clear pictures anywhere there is enough light to see clearly—and natural-looking pictures even where the light is too dim to see clearly.

This paradox arises from the limitations of human vision. What looks normal in a photograph depends on what the eye sees as normal under similar conditions. Although human vision adjusts for the great range of brightness between summer sunlight and feeble candlelight, below that lower limit it cannot compensate fully for lessened illumination—scenes look dim, the shadows lacking in detail. To reproduce this appearance, the camera, like the eye, should not compensate fully for the lack of light—and the new combination of lenses and film do not.

This new ability to match the sensitivity of human vision makes photography as fast as most people want it. Greater speed would create serious problems of overexposure for shots in sunlight unless extremely high shutter speeds were used. Smaller f-stops on the lens aperture would not help, for an opening much smaller than the f/16 now provided on most 110 cameras would blur the image—light waves squeezing through a hole that small interfere with one another.

Such limitations do not hem in what might be called the electronification of the camera; the newest models are almost totally automated by electronic devices. The takeover of such automation has been rapid, beginning almost two decades ago with the use of a transistor and photoelectric cell to adjust shutter speed for correct exposure. This early, rather single-minded automation—disdained by professionals—has now evolved into a marvelously diverse, multifunctioned system that releases professionals and amateurs alike from the drudgery of normal settings.

The electronic camera became possible with the advent of so-called integrated circuits—entire working systems of transistors and other electronic components etched onto chips, each the size of a flyspeck. The chips are small enough to fit into a camera and capable enough to act as specialized computers. They measure illumination, remember film speed, calculate diaphragm and shutter settings as well as distance, keep track of time, count signals, send and receive electrical pulses and turn signal lights on and off. The chip computers enabled camera controls to become digital, operating with specific, discrete numbers rather than gradually varying voltages—a change that reduces errors and increases versatility.

One bonus of digital electronic controls is automatic focusing, which becomes more valuable as speed goes up for work in weak light. In dim light, automatic focusing is more accurate than the human eye. And accuracy is vital in low illumination, for there the lens is used at its widest diaphragm setting, which gives least depth of field—the distance over which acceptable sharpness is attained.

Through electronic automation, precision has been brought to inexpensive cameras and has been made more flexible in expensive ones. The snapshooter now can make technically superior pictures without increased effort and the advanced photographer can relieve himself of the mundane. Today's electronics is evolving so rapidly that the next major step may be to a new photographic technology—as electronic as television but with the quality of film.

Cameras That Think

by Mel Ingber

Mel Ingber, the author of this article and the three following in The New Technology section, is a freelance writer on photography.

The 1936 Contax III was the first camera with a built-in light meter, a rectangular box that was mounted above the lens but was not connected to either diaphragm or shutter.

Until now cameras have been made like fine watches, with springs, gears and levers. Today the camera, like the watch, has been transformed. Outwardly it looks only slightly different, but inside is a computer. Mechanical parts have given way to electronic ones.

In 1978 two new cameras, the Canon A-1 and the Konica FS-1, made the "electronification" of the camera nearly complete. With a flick of a switch on the Canon A-1 (page 155) the photographer can choose to control exposure automatically with the diaphragm, the shutter or both, or he can control exposure manually. In the Konica FS-1 (pages 138-139), a motorized system automatically loads film and advances it for each exposure.

What makes the Canon A-1 and Konica FS-1 remarkable, however, is that they think. Each contains an electronic brain—a central processing unit, or CPU—that keeps track of what is happening, decides what should happen next and activates the circuits to make it happen.

Over the years electronics has affected the camera in three significant areas—in light meters, in the control of diaphragms and shutters, and in the linkages coordinating the camera's functions. In the 1930s, light meters became the first electronic element added to a camera. Their light sensors, mounted near the camera lens, were selenium cells, which generate a tiny electrical current when light falls on them, moving an indicator needle. But the current varies with light intensity; in dim light the current is so small that large cells are needed.

In the 1960s cells of cadmium sulfide (CdS), 1,000 times more sensitive than selenium and thus much smaller, took over. The CdS cell acts as a valve, regulating the flow of electricity between a battery and the meter. The brighter the light shining on the cells, the greater the current and the higher the meter reading. High sensitivity made the CdS cell small enough to be placed within the camera behind the lens, where it could measure the brightness of the light that would expose the film. Today cameras such as the new Konica have even smaller and more efficient cells of silicon or gallium arsenide phosphide. Like selenium, they generate current rather than control flow, but weak current in dim light can be strengthened by minuscule electronic amplifiers inside the camera.

The first meters were linked to the camera by the photographer, who read the dial and set the shutter and diaphragm. But once the exposure meter had become part of the camera, it could be linked directly to the camera's exposure controls, eliminating the photographer-middleman. Some cameras automated only the diaphragm; others automated only the shutter control; others automated both.

Until the introduction of cameras controlled by electronics, all automated aperture controls worked on the same principle: the meter needle reading the illumination of the scene freezes at the measurement it makes when the shutter-release button is pressed, and through a mechanical linkage determines the diaphragm opening. Because this trap-needle system depends on a special linkage between the shutter release and the diaphragm, it did not work readily in

Automation appeared in the Super Kodak Six-20 of 1938, which had an exposure meter geared directly to the diaphragm.

The 1959 Agfa Optima pioneered fully automatic control with an exposure meter geared to diaphragm and shutter.

In 1963, through-the-lens light metering was introduced in this Topcon, which set tiny CdS cells behind slits in the viewfinder mirror.

The 1967 Konica Autoreflex-T was the first professional-quality camera with through-the-lens metering controlling the diaphragm.

SLRs: making the linkage to the diaphragm—inside the lens—proved complicated in cameras that were intended to have removable, interchangeable lenses. Manufacturers of most SLRs turned to exposure control through shutters.

Automated shutter control had to wait for the transistor, whose small size made it possible to incorporate within the confines of the camera body amplifying, regulating and switching devices that adjust the length of time the two "curtains" of a focal-plane shutter remain open. When the shutter button is pressed, releasing the first curtain, current from a battery flows through a CdS cell, which regulates the amount passed according to the light available. The current goes to a capacitor, a sort of electrical bank, where electric charge builds up until a predetermined amount is reached. At that point, a transistor triggers a magnetic catch to let go of the second curtain. In this way the brightness of light controls the rate at which the charge builds, and thus the time the shutter is open.

The latest automation circuitry, such as that used in the new Konica and Canon, is an outgrowth of computer technology. For computers to become more versatile without becoming larger, it was necessary to develop electronic components of smaller and smaller size. Scientists found ways to produce in a single operation integrated circuits of microscopic transistors, resistors, capacitors, switches and all their interconnections. Integrated circuits control the camera's functions from one central command post. Instead of one operation mechanically triggering the next, the various operations are now coordinated by a central processing unit. As orders from the CPU flow over printed circuits and wires to satellite switches and motors that activate shutters and diaphragms, fewer and fewer mechanical connections are needed. The light meter, for example, has lost its needle; voltage from the meter cell is now interpreted by an integrated circuit that combines it with information from shutter-speed or aperture dials to determine exposure.

Also inherited from computers is a new system of shutter timing that uses a built-in digital clock instead of a capacitor. The clock counts pulses of electricity until a preselected time is reached. Digital techniques are also used to calculate exposure. The integrated circuit that interprets the light meter's readings converts voltages to patterns of pulses and uses them in computations. The reliability of the computations is greatly increased—since pulse patterns, unlike voltages themselves, are unaffected by changes in temperature and humidity. Such digital circuits also control lens movement in automatic-focusing cameras like the Polaroid SX-70 (pages 140-143).

It is even conceivable that mechanical shutters and diaphragms may one day be replaced by electronic elements that make the lens switch from opaque to transparent. And the film itself may disappear when silver-halide emulsions are replaced by an electronic memory.

Inside the Konica's Brain

Because it was designed as a complete electronic system, the Konica FS-1 combines in centralized units some of the functions that were once handled by individual controls. Thus, several integrated circuits, two motors and four magnetic switches operate the film-wind, the shutter, the viewing mirror and the diaphragm *(right)*.

Probably the most impressive of all these unified electronic subsystems is the Konica's digital brain—its CPU, or central processing unit. With more than 1,100 "gates," or electronic switches, and 250 transistors, the CPU monitors and directs information to and from each of the camera's functioning parts. Indeed, the CPU can even override the photographer if he makes a mistake in setting and, using its own judgment, can set the controls correctly.

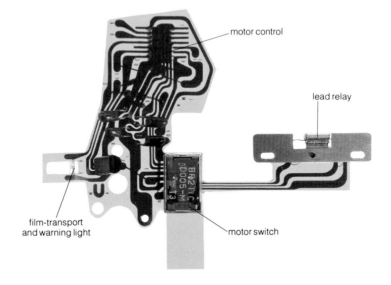

motor control

lead relay

film-transport and warning light

motor switch

Automatic film loading and winding on the new Konica camera is controlled by the circuitry at left. When the film is inserted and the back of the camera is closed, a switch turns on the film-winding motor and advances the film to the first frame. After each exposure, the central processing unit signals the motor control to advance the film to the next frame. The lead relay monitors film tension; when a tight pull indicates the film has reached the end of the roll or has jammed, this relay turns off the motor and turns on a warning light. The same light blinks when the film is being advanced, to show that it is loaded properly.

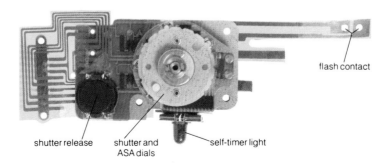

flash contact

shutter release

shutter and ASA dials

self-timer light

Gathered together in the unit at left are the electronic components of the Konica's shutter dial, film-speed (ASA) dial, shutter release, self-timer and flash contact. From this unit, located under a panel on top of the camera (photograph below), information flows to and from the central processing unit. The flash connection, for example, tells the CPU what aperture the flash unit has been set for, and the CPU informs the flash unit of the speed of the film being used. Through this connection, the CPU also determines when the flash has not recharged; it then switches the camera back to automatic exposure, without flash, so that photographs will not be improperly exposed.

shutter and ASA dials

shutter release

flash contact

self-timer light

The Konica FS-1 (left) even looks different from nonelectronic cameras. There is no film-advance lever, and it has a hand-grip bulge on the left front—the built-in chamber for the four penlight batteries powering the camera circuits. The battery chamber can be detached and kept warm inside the photographer's pocket in extremely cold weather, to prevent the voltage reduction that can be caused by low temperatures.

In place of the gear wheels and levers that open and close the two curtains of a focal-plane shutter on a conventional camera (far right), the FS-1 has two electrically operated magnetic switches—the plastic-encased, copper-colored elements visible at near right. Shutter timing is regulated by a digital clock in the central processing unit. Digital timing, unaffected by adverse atmospheric conditions, makes the shutter much more accurate.

 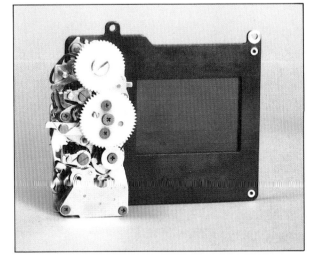

The Konica's multifunctional viewfinder is packed with information. Besides focusing aids—a split image, microprism ring and ground-glass circle—an aperture scale runs along one edge, flanked by lights to signal what is going on inside the camera. The top light goes on when the aperture is selected manually; others indicate the correct aperture, whether selected manually or automatically. In addition, four lights blink as well as glow. The second from the top blinks to warn of underexposure, the one at the bottom to warn of overexposure. If both lights blink alternately, batteries need changing. The lights f/5.6 and f/11 also blink when the flash unit is ready.

Focusing with Inaudible Chirps

The newest development in camera automation—automatic focusing—has now been incorporated into instant cameras. Unlike previous devices, which use light to measure distance, Polaroid's Sonar sends out a burst of sound and "listens" for an echo from the subject, like the mechanisms employed by submarines and bats. The greater the distance to the subject, the longer it takes for the sound to return, and this interval of time determines the camera's focus. Versions of the system are used in both the SX-70 and Pronto cameras; the SX-70 system is described here, but both are the same in principle.

The Polaroid Sonar system is ultrasonic—it uses sound more than twice as high in pitch, or frequency, as the human ear can hear—working in the same frequency range as bats, between 50,000 and 60,000 cycles per second. The burst of sound lasts for only .001 second, and travels at a speed of about 1,090 feet per second, taking .036 second to reach and return from an object 20 feet away. For a close-up object 10.4 inches away—as close as the camera can focus—the round-trip time is .0016 second.

The devices that transmit, receive and time this burst of sound and then use the accumulated information to set the lens position are a sophisticated blend of electronic, optical and mechanical components. The most visible of them is the combination loudspeaker-microphone that emits the sound and receives the echo. Its central element is a vibrating circular membrane of gold-plated plastic film that sends out a chirp of sound composed, in rapid succession, of four different frequencies. Four tones are needed in case one or more of them is absorbed or canceled out by an unusual pattern of reflections. After delivering the chirp, the loudspeaker turns off for a fraction of a second to let the vibrations die out. Then it switches on again, but as a microphone, to await the returning echo. The longer the microphone has to wait before catching the echo, the more sensitive its receiving circuitry becomes, to compensate for the weakened signal of sound returning from a distant subject.

The source of the chirps sent out by the loudspeaker-microphone is the system's master clock. It is a circuit, like those in digital watches, that generates high-frequency oscillations to make the chirps as well as electrical pulses, or "ticks," to time the length of the sound wave's trip. The ticks begin when the chirp is emitted and end when the echo returns. They are stored by a counter that can record up to 128 ticks—representing the range of 128 zones of focus for the lens. The more distant the subject, the longer it takes the echo to return and the greater the number of ticks that are counted.

When the distance has been measured in this way, the clock turns off and the lens-positioning motor turns on, moving the lens from its "park" setting a bit beyond the infinity setting. This movement is also monitored by the counter, which now picks up electrical pulses from a different source—a slotted lens-count wheel that rotates as the lens changes its setting. The wheel passes between a tiny light and a photoelectric cell that converts the blinks of light produced by the slots into pulses

A compact unit atop the camera contains the automatic focusing system of the new Polaroid Sonar SX-70. The most visible element, a gold disc on the front, is the loudspeaker-microphone that sends sonic chirps and receives echoes.

With front and back covers removed, the Sonar's automatic focusing system presents a colorful array of mechanical and electronic parts that together control three separate operations — sending, receiving, and focusing — described in detail on pages 142-143. The loudspeaker-microphone and clock (bottom) generate sound chirps and receive and time echoes, the filters eliminate false echoes and the amplifier strengthens the echo. In the focusing phase the motor moves the lens; the counter, lens-count wheel and magnetic latch stop the lens at the point of sharp focus.

magnetic latch — lens-count wheel

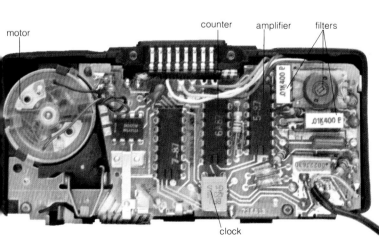

motor — counter — amplifier — filters — clock

loudspeaker-microphone

of electricity. When the counter has accumulated a total of 128 pulses from both sources, the SX-70 is in focus and the usual picturetaking cycle starts. At the completion of the cycle, the focusing system once again takes over and returns the lens to park.

Polaroid's system allows for variations in focus requirements. When the subject is just a few feet away, very few clock ticks will be needed to record distance, leaving most of the 128 spaces in the counter to be filled by pulses from the lens-count wheel as it moves the lens into sharp focus. The system takes into account that focus is more critical for near subjects than for distant ones; most of the 128 lens positions are concentrated in this close-in region, where greater precision is needed. Conversely, when the subject is 30 feet away or beyond, a distance at which all of the 128 spaces in the counter will be occupied by clock ticks, the lens of the SX-70 automatically focuses at 30 feet, making sharp everything from 28 feet on.

The new focusing system works in dim light or no light at all; because it "sees" with sound it can be used to take flash pictures in a totally darkened room. It does, however, have limitations. One is its inability to focus on anything except objects at the center of the viewfinder. To overcome this drawback, Polaroid has added a two-stage shutter release that permits the photographer to center the desired subject, depress the shutter partway to focus correctly, then aim the camera again to frame the subject as desired. After the picture has been recomposed, the shutter action is completed.

The new system also will not work when obstacles such as windows and screens lie between the camera and the subject; the chirp bounces off them, focusing the camera on the obstacle rather than the scene beyond. And its performance may be affected by cold, rarified atmospheres. In such conditions, sound travels at a slower rate than normal, and may cause the SX-70 to focus slightly beyond the point desired—although Polaroid tests indicate that short of the cold, rarified atmosphere of Mt. Everest, this effect is negligible. In any situation where the ultrasonic system is fooled by conditions such as these, the camera can be switched to manual focusing—giving the photographer the option of taking pictures in the old familiar ways, without the benefit of advanced technology.

Steps to Sharp Focus

In the .036 second it takes the Polaroid system to focus on a subject 20 feet away, its components move through three distinct modes of operation—one for sending out chirps of sound, a second for receiving the returning echo and a third for focusing the lens. The components that are operating during each of these stages appear in color in the three diagrams at right.

Below each diagram is a bar graph indicating how the system counter records electrical pulses through each of the three modes of operation. During the first two modes—sending and receiving—the pulses tick off the passage of time, measuring the amount of time it takes for the sound burst to reach and return from the subject, represented here by a rose. In the third mode of operation, the pulses indicate the distance traveled by the lens as it moves.

The counter is programed to accept only 128 pulses, and it stops the lens movement when the 128th pulse arrives. For distant subjects most of the counter's record will be occupied by pulses measuring time, leaving very few for lens motion. When the subject is closer at hand, most of the spaces in the counter will record the action of the lens as it moves into sharp focus.

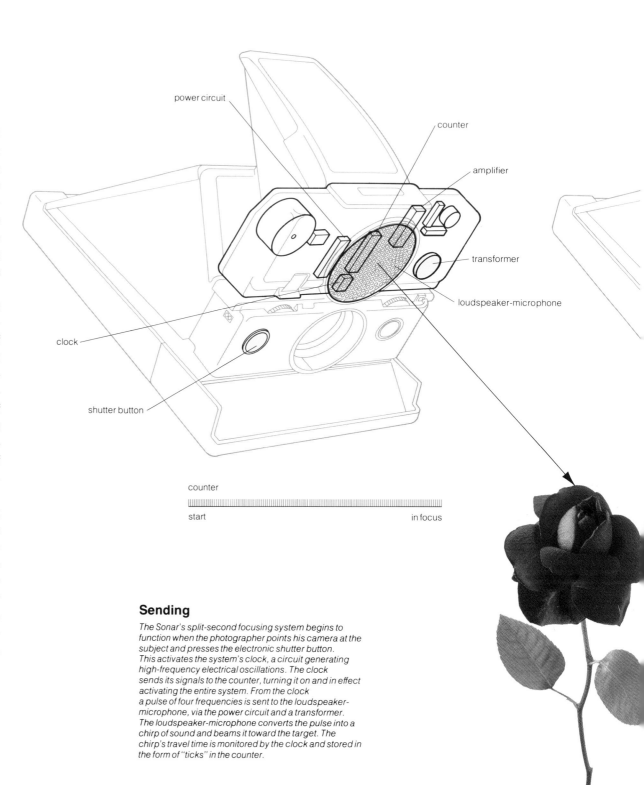

counter

start   in focus

Sending

The Sonar's split-second focusing system begins to function when the photographer points his camera at the subject and presses the electronic shutter button. This activates the system's clock, a circuit generating high-frequency electrical oscillations. The clock sends its signals to the counter, turning it on and in effect activating the entire system. From the clock a pulse of four frequencies is sent to the loudspeaker-microphone, via the power circuit and a transformer. The loudspeaker-microphone converts the pulse into a chirp of sound and beams it toward the target. The chirp's travel time is monitored by the clock and stored in the form of "ticks" in the counter.

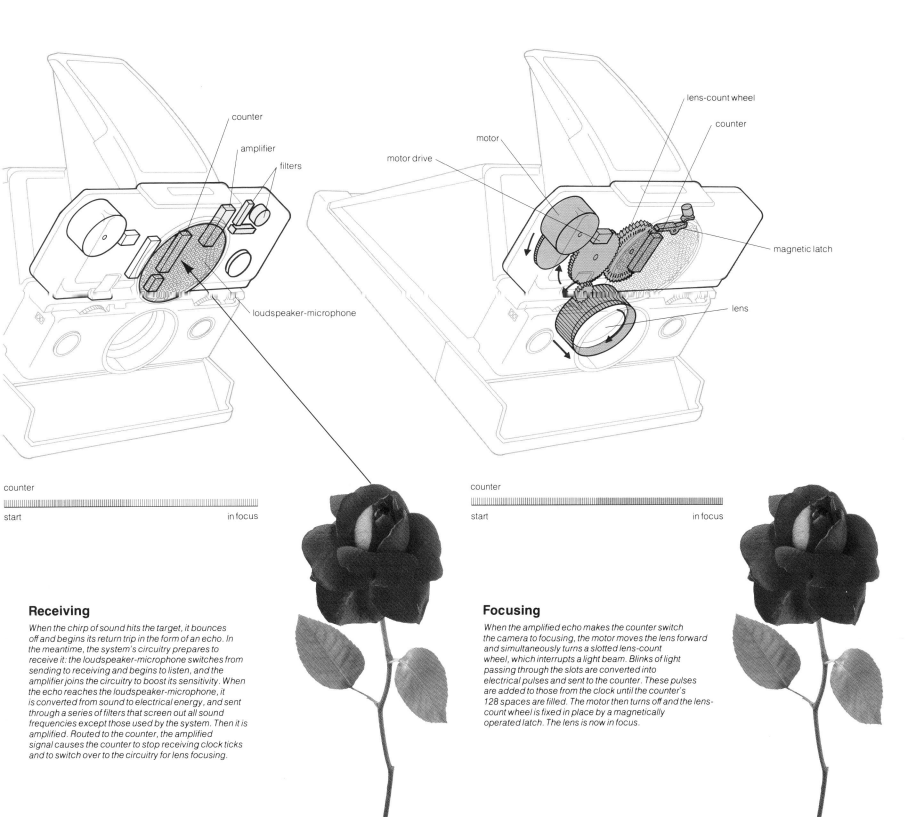

counter

start   in focus

Receiving

When the chirp of sound hits the target, it bounces off and begins its return trip in the form of an echo. In the meantime, the system's circuitry prepares to receive it: the loudspeaker-microphone switches from sending to receiving and begins to listen, and the amplifier joins the circuitry to boost its sensitivity. When the echo reaches the loudspeaker-microphone, it is converted from sound to electrical energy, and sent through a series of filters that screen out all sound frequencies except those used by the system. Then it is amplified. Routed to the counter, the amplified signal causes the counter to stop receiving clock ticks and to switch over to the circuitry for lens focusing.

counter

start   in focus

Focusing

When the amplified echo makes the counter switch the camera to focusing, the motor moves the lens forward and simultaneously turns a slotted lens-count wheel, which interrupts a light beam. Blinks of light passing through the slots are converted into electrical pulses and sent to the counter. These pulses are added to those from the clock until the counter's 128 spaces are filled. The motor then turns off and the lens-count wheel is fixed in place by a magnetically operated latch. The lens is now in focus.

An Aspherical Lens—Speed at Low Cost

A fast lens never before obtainable on a popularly priced camera helps the new Kodak Ektramax 110 to deliver high-quality photographs in dim light. The Ektramax lens, which must meet demanding requirements of sharpness to produce detailed pictures from the tiny images of 110-size film, has a maximum aperture of f/1.9, an opening previously found only on 110-format cameras selling for nearly twice the price. Partly by making three of the lens' four elements of plastic instead of glass, the cost of the camera was held below $90. But the real technical achievement in the new lens is that one of these plastic elements is aspherical: that is, its surface does not have the uniform curvature of a sphere, as do nearly all other photographic lenses. Instead, the curvature makes a slight wiggle near the edge. A sophisticated approach to lens quality, traditionally expensive and rarely used, the aspherical lens has been transformed by Kodak into an inexpensive, mass-produced part.

The aspherical lens is the obvious solution to a problem inherent to spherical lenses (called, in fact, spherical aberration). The evenly curved spherical lens bends too sharply the light rays passing through the area near the edge of the lens; as a result, the rays meet at a point on the film slightly removed from those passing through the center of the lens *(diagram at right)*. This displacement blurs the image.

There are several common methods for correcting spherical aberration. The lens can be stopped down to a smaller opening, blocking the troublesome light rays from the edges—but this also decreases the lens' light-gathering power. In a typical modern lens, made up of five or more complementary single lens elements, designers build in correction by including among the convex elements a concave one to cancel out, with its opposite curvature, the spherical aberration introduced by the convex elements. This, however, adds cost, size and weight to the lens and the camera. The aspherical lens solves the problem by incorporating corrective curvature into the surface of an otherwise convex lens, making the outer portion less convex than the center, or even concave—the actual shape depending on the light-bending properties of the other elements in the lens.

For all the obvious advantages of the aspherical lens, its use has been limited by the difficulty—and high cost—of manufacturing it. Unlike spherical surfaces, whose even curvatures can be produced easily on simple grinding machines, aspherical surfaces have curvatures that are different at different points and require complex production methods. From concept to fabrication, a piece of aspherical glass requires a maze of mathematical calculations that can tax the imagination and patience of even the most skillful optical physicist. Although high-speed computers have simplified this aspect of lens design in recent years, and most of the grinding and polishing of the glass also is now done with computer-guided tools, aspherical surfaces still pose formidable problems.

For all the difficulties aspherical lenses involve, they have been popular with optical designers since 1930, when an Estonian instrument maker, Bernhard Schmidt, incorporated an aspherical corrective plate into a mirror telescope. Since then, aspherical lens elements have been used in more conventional but very

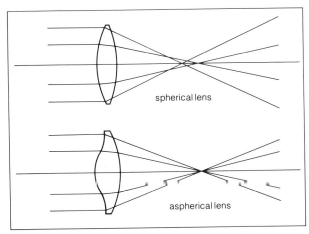

This schematic comparison of the even curvature of a spherical lens (top) and the undulating surface of an aspherical lens shows how the shape of each lens affects the path of light rays passing through it. Light rays that pass through areas near the edges of the spherical lens do not focus at the same point as those that pass through the middle. The aspherical lens has a surface less convex near the rim than it is at the center to bend the peripheral light rays less, thus causing all rays to converge at the same point and producing a perfectly focused image.

expensive lens assemblies to make fast-zoom and wide-angle lenses for movie cameras. And in 1972 Canon introduced a mass-produced aspherical element into some of its lenses for 35mm still cameras. But these Canon lenses, selling for about $1,000 each, are beyond the means of all but the most affluent photographers.

All that changed this year, when Kodak found a way to mass-produce aspherical lenses inexpensively from plastic. Plastic lenses have been common for more than two decades. Like toys and TV knobs, they are made by a process called injection molding (*page 146*). The trick to making them is, of course, the mold. For a flawless product, the mold must not change size as temperature changes, and it must be machined to the exact shape of the lens. In addition, it has to take a high polish so that it produces an optically smooth surface, and it must have good heat-transfer qualities—that is, it has to heat and cool evenly to avoid straining the plastic.

Those requirements apply to all lens molds, spherical or aspherical, and they had already been solved by the use of a special ceramic. The new problem was shape—machining the mold to a curvature with the desired wiggle, then testing the mold and the lenses it produced to make sure the wiggle was correct. The testing required, in addition to computers, such devices from the frontiers of optical science as holograms—the complex optical patterns that can create three-dimensional images—and laser beams. With their aid, it became possible to check the curvatures of molds and lenses, which deviate from a sphere by only a few hundredths of a thousandth of an inch, by employing an interferometer, the optical device long used for ultraprecise measurements.

In the interferometer used to test aspherical lenses, light from a single source is split into two beams. One beam is bounced, unaltered, off a mirror; the lens under test reflects the second beam, whose light waves are altered by the lens curvature. The second beam also passes through a null corrector—a device that undoes the light-wave alterations introduced by the lens surface. This null corrector causes light-wave changes exactly opposite to those introduced by a perfect lens. Thus, when the second beam bounces off a perfect lens and then passes through the null corrector, it will be identical to the first beam. But if the second beam bounces off an imperfect lens, the null corrector cannot make it identical to the first beam.

The difference between matching and unmatching beams—perfect and imperfect lenses—is made visible in patterns cast on the interferometer viewing screen. Identical beams, indicating a perfect lens, create a pattern of even stripes; mismatched beams, indicating an imperfect lens, produce an irregular pattern.

For the precise measurement that lenses and lens molds require, the light beams must contain light of a single wavelength, and for this purpose lasers are used. To work with the null corrector, engineers included a hologram; its pattern—generated by a computer—creates no image but distorts laser light waves to help form a standard of accurate aspherical curvature against which lenses and molds can be checked. The result of all this 21st Century technology is an ultrafast lens of high quality at a price no one had dreamed possible.

Making the Lens

Although the advantage of aspherical lenses has been recognized for many years, the key to producing them at low cost was sophisticated plastics and mold-making technology. Kodak keeps its lens-making techniques a secret, but the method is known to be a refinement of the injection molding process used to mass-produce the conventional plastic lens. In Kodak's process, warm, melted plastic with optical properties similar to those of glass is squeezed into a ceramic mold. The mold has tubular channels that end in eight compartments, each having the shape of the lens. After the plastic has been injected into the mold, it cools and hardens within minutes.

An eight-lens mold can turn out hundreds of lenses per hour, and each mold can be used to make hundreds of thousands of lenses before it needs to be replaced.

A Kodak inspector looks for obvious imperfections in a set of eight aspherical lens elements fresh from the injection molding press. The connecting material between the lenses is plastic that hardened in the tubular channels through which the molds are filled. After the lens elements are separated from the connecting plastic, one aspherical element is installed into each of the Ektramax lenses.

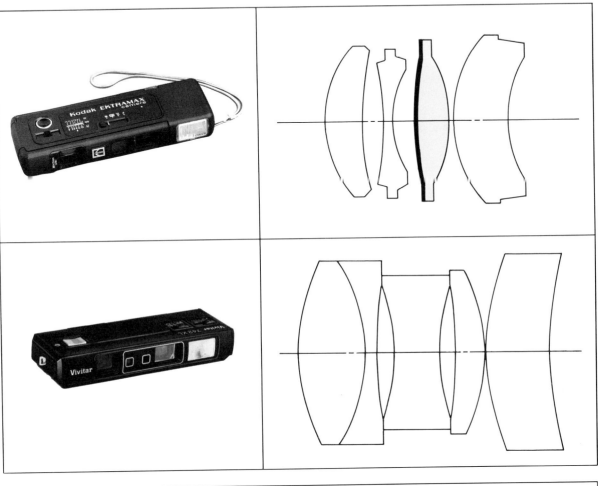

The Kodak Ektramax 110 camera (far left) is the first 110 using an aspherically shaped plastic lens element to provide an f/1.9 lens. Its price: about $90. The lens, shown in the diagram, consists of only four elements, three plastic and, to their left, one glass. One of the plastic elements is aspherical (blue tint). On its front surface (heavy line), the outer areas are less convex than center ones; this aspherical curvature, unlike a spherical one, focuses both outer and central rays at the same point to create a sharp image.

The Vivitar 742 XL (far left), introduced in 1977, has a standard f/1.9 lens that, until 1978, was the only lens of this speed available for use with 110 film. Five spherical lens elements were needed to counter lens aberrations. So many elements and the fact that they are all glass helped push the camera's cost to about $190.

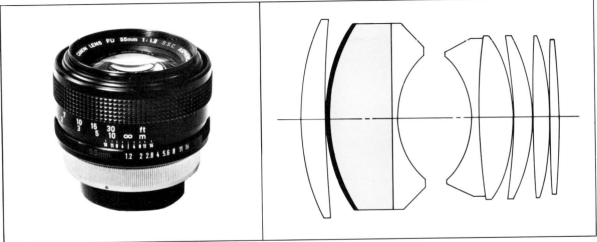

Until 1978, the only camera lenses made with aspherical elements were expensive glass designs for professionals, such as this Canon 55mm model (far left), which costs about $1,200. It has eight lens elements, including one (blue tint) with one aspherical surface (heavy line). It is very fast: f/1.2.

Slide Film Twice as Fast, No Grainier

The latest in a succession of dramatic developments that have radically altered color photography during the past decade made its debut in 1978. It is Kodak's high-speed slide film, Ektachrome 400, a film rated at ASA 400, twice as fast as those available just a year ago and about eight times as fast as the slide films of 20 years ago. With the new Ektachrome and the equally fast print films introduced in 1977, anyone can take indoor color pictures without flash, and outdoor action shots without blurring. Ordinary room light gives adequate exposure at normal lens and shutter settings. Outdoors, 1/500-second or faster shutter settings can freeze motion even in dim light.

High speed in a film normally implies a trade-off in other aspects of picture quality, notably graininess—for it is an annoying axiom of photo physics that the faster the film, the larger its image-capturing crystals must be. But pictures made with the new film have a grain comparable to that of much slower types. This remarkable achievement is partly the result of a long succession of improvements in film quality dating back into the last century. But mainly, it is the product of recent innovations in film manufacture that permit the plastic film base to be coated with multiple layers of microscopically thin emulsion. By varying the density and viscosity of adjacent layers, many layers now can be applied simultaneously—at a great saving in production time and cost. This advance in coating technique brings design flexibility that enables fast but grainy emulsions to be combined with fine-grained but slow emulsions to produce a fast film that does not appear grainy.

The ASA 400 film is composed of 11 separate layers of emulsion, each a few ten-thousandths of an inch thick and each carrying a different set of chemicals, providing scientists 11 different components to juggle and manipulate. To understand how film designers have used this unprecedented array of chemical variables, it is necessary to understand some of the basic principles of image formation in photographic materials.

Emulsions for both color and black-and-white films are based on a group of compounds known as silver halides—mainly silver bromide and silver iodide—which are transformed by light and developing chemicals into silver metal, the black of a black-and-white photographic image. The halides are crystalline in form, as snowflakes are, but smaller—less than 1/10,000 inch across. Over the years, in the course of many experiments, scientists have improved the light-recording power of these crystals in several distinct ways. One is by enlarging the size of the crystals.

When a particle of light, called a photon, enters a film, there is a much better chance of its hitting large crystals than small ones, simply because the target area is bigger. Large crystals, however, cannot record as much detail as small ones—their resolution is less. And they are lumpier than small ones. This lumpiness shows up as graininess, a mottling effect in the developed image. Both loss of detail and lumpiness are particular problems today because the most popular film sizes, 135 (35mm), 126 and 110, require high magnification for viewing.

Another way to increase the crystals' sensitivity to light is to alter their structure so

Shown above in actual size is one of three 35mm transparencies—identical views of the Washington Monument from across the Potomac River—that were used to make the film comparison shown opposite. This transparency was made with the new high-speed, fine-grained Ektachrome 400 film; the other two with Ektachrome 200 and Ektachrome 64, which are, respectively, one half and one fourth as sensitive to light.

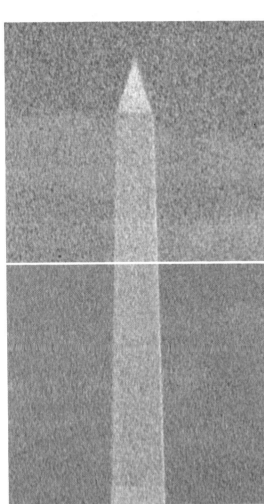

In this 30X enlargement of the view reproduced on page 148, a three-tiered composite of the Washington Monument has been formed by combining parts of three photographs, each taken from the identical spot but on films of three different speeds. The section at the top, made on the very fast ASA 400 film, is remarkably close in picture quality to that of the slower ASA 200 film, which was used for the middle section. Only the very slow ASA 64 film, used for the bottom section, gives distinctly greater definition and detail.

that the pattern formed by their atoms is less regular, creating what physicists call traps; it is in these traps that metallic silver atoms collect when the film is exposed. The traps must be strong enough to hold light-affected silver atoms until the film is processed, but at the same time vulnerable enough to be accessible to the developer, which completes the transformation of silver halide into silver metal.

These traps can be created in crystals by changes in temperature or in chemical composition when the crystals are grown, or by adding impurities to the materials that compose the crystals. Only when scientists began to understand the role played by impurity traps did they find that sulfur increased the sensitivity of silver halides. (The discovery came about when differences in speed among emulsion batches were traced to the diets of the cows whose hides and bones provided gelatin for the emulsion—the speed was faster if the forage contained minute amounts of sulfur.) Later, in the 1930s, gold was found to have a similar effect. Today many different impurities are introduced in precise ways to affect crystal structure, and other methods also are used. Details of any of these methods are fragmentary, for film scientists are reluctant to explain processes involving valuable proprietary information. They speak guardedly of "concentrating image-forming atoms to enhance their light sensitivity," or even more guardedly of using "good emulsion technology."

Finally, there are ways to improve the crystals' sensitivity to light by expanding the kind of light they respond to. Silver halides alone have very little sensitivity to light other than in wavelengths of blue. But by the 1870s it was found that adding dyes to the emulsion made the crystals respond to green and yellow light. In 1905, a red-sensitizing dye was also discovered. When added to an emulsion, the dyes adhere to the silver-halide crystals and, on exposure to light, absorb colors not absorbed by the crystals. Then the dyes react with the crystals, producing the same effect on them as if the crystals had been directly exposed. In that way, they make colors other than blue initiate the transformation of silver halide to silver metal.

Although sensitizing dyes are obviously essential to color photography—without them red and green would show up as black—they are different in character from the dyes that form the final color image in color film; for one thing, the sensitizing dyes disappear during processing. Most color film is composed basically of three sections of light-sensitive emulsion, responsive respectively to blue, green and red. Each section contains silver-halide crystals plus molecules called color couplers, which become dye in the final image. During processing the developer reacts first with the crystals, changing them into grains of metallic silver. Then it migrates and reacts with the surrounding color couplers, forming nimbus-like clouds of dye around each grain of silver. In the 1950s this basic three-section color film was subdivided into six layers, each color acquiring two layers—one fast layer, with big grains; the other slow and fine-grained. For the new Ektachrome, seven layers are provided: three each to record red and green, one for blue. This method of separation gave scientists a new freedom. They could now control, layer by layer, the concentration and type of color coupler in each, and by readjusting the proportion of couplers to crystals, they could minimize the visible effects of graininess in the fast layers.

To make graininess less obvious, scientists relied on the long-known fact that the human eye tolerates loss of detail in the shadowy areas of an image far more easily than it does in the middle tones. In effect, people do not expect to see as well in the dark. Taking advantage of this characteristic, scientists began to manipulate the size and density of the dye clouds in the final image of the fast emulsion layers, so as to make graininess less apparent.

To achieve high speed, the fast emulsion was made very fast through the use of large silver-halide crystals. To minimize the graininess they create, the concentration of dye coupler was limited. This forces the developer to wander relatively great distances to find couplers to react with. In addition, a relatively unreactive coupler was used, further increasing the distance the developer has to wander before it and a coupler collide energetically enough to form the dye. Because the developer must wander so far to be effective, it creates large, overlapping dye clouds to make the image. The result is a diffuse image, lacking in sharp detail, in the shadows—where loss of sharpness is tolerated by human vision.

In the brighter parts of the picture, the image is created by the slower, finer-grained emulsions. The fast, grainy layer does not interfere with those parts of the image—in those areas, processing has made the fast layer essentially transparent. In print films, this process is carried even further and is called coupler starvation.

For print films—but not for slide films—another development in color couplers helps to combat graininess. It is called a developer-inhibitor-releasing coupler, DIR coupler for short, and it makes a high-speed, large-crystal emulsion produce the fine grains usually found only in a slow emulsion. Part of the chemical package of each DIR coupler molecule is a detachable segment that can prevent the developer from reacting with the silver-halide crystals. During color formation, these inhibitors are released from the coupler, and their presence in the neighborhood interferes with the full development of the crystals. The lack of development of a portion of a crystal does not alter the intensity of the color, because a fully developed crystal can produce more dye than needed. It does, however, reduce the size of the dye cloud, producing from large crystals a semblance of the fine grain associated with small-crystal emulsions. The DIR coupler, because it reduces the size of the dye cloud, also permits more crystals to be introduced into the emulsion, thereby increasing its sensitivity.

All of these advances in light detection and color formation, together with recent achievements in emulsion coating, contributed to the new high-speed color films. Indeed, the ASA 400 films may signal a new generation of color photography. Although the films are rated at ASA 400, they can be "pushed" to greater speed by exposing them as if their rating were ASA 800 or even ASA 1600. Such speeds are as fast as anyone is likely to want color film to be for ordinary photography.

protective coating
blue-sensitive layer
yellow filter
green-sensitive fast layer
green-sensitive medium-speed layer
green-sensitive slow layer
interlayer
red-sensitive fast layer
red-sensitive medium-speed layer
red-sensitive slow layer
antihalation layer
base

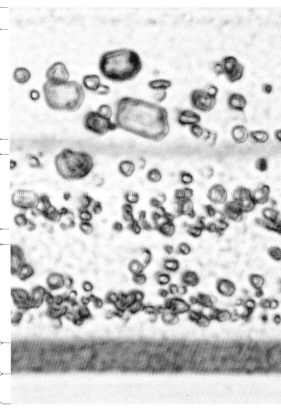

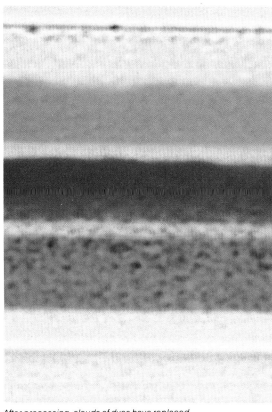

A cross section of Ektachrome 400 film identifies the working layers between the plastic base and a scratch-resistant coating. At top is a blue-sensitive emulsion containing silver-halide crystals and color coupler that turns this layer yellow. Beneath it, a yellow filter blocks blue light. Next, three tiers of green-sensitive emulsion contain magenta dye coupler and three sizes of silver-halide crystals, the second and third progressively less sensitive but finer in grain than the first. Below an interlayer, a three-tiered red-sensitive emulsion contains three sizes of crystals and dye couplers that create cyan. The antihalation layer absorbs reflections in the film.

A photograph of unexposed Ektachrome 400 film reveals the actual appearance of the emulsion layers. The single blue-sensitive layer contains crystals of various sizes—the resulting graininess is camouflaged by the yellow dye it produces. The green-sensitive emulsion has large crystals at its top, giving high speed and relatively large grains; in the middle are medium-sized crystals for medium speed and graininess; at bottom are primarily small crystals, slower but finer-grained. The red-sensitive emulsion has three tiers like those in the green-sensitive emulsion.

After processing, clouds of dyes have replaced silver-halide crystals and the layers in the film have shrunk together. During projection each of these dyes blocks a different part of the spectrum and allows the complementary color to pass; thus the yellow dye passes blue, the magenta green and the cyan red. This film was left unexposed for demonstration purposes; if it had been exposed, each layer would contain variations in shade to create the image.

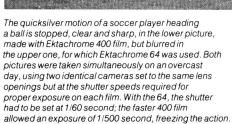

The quicksilver motion of a soccer player heading a ball is stopped, clear and sharp, in the lower picture, made with Ektachrome 400 film, but blurred in the upper one, for which Ektachrome 64 was used. Both pictures were taken simultaneously on an overcast day, using two identical cameras set to the same lens openings but at the shutter speeds required for proper exposure on each film. With the 64, the shutter had to be set at 1/60 second; the faster 400 film allowed an exposure of 1/500 second, freezing the action.

Indoors, the advantages of the high-speed film are as tempting as they are outdoors, but color rendition may be affected, as these two pictures demonstrate. The picture at top, made in a photography gallery with 64 film, required a flash, resulting in a picture so unevenly illuminated that the features of the young woman in the foreground are washed out by the bright light, and shadow details in the ceiling are lost. In the lower picture, the same scene photographed with an identical camera on 400 film without flash, using only available light, is evenly lit and better detailed. However, because Ektachrome 400 is color-balanced for daylight or flash, not artificial light, the tones in this picture are warmer than usual.

Cameras and Equipment

Pentax 110 SLR with Motor Drive

Streamlined 110s

The growing popularity of the small-format 110 prompted the introduction of six new models in 1978, most of them sophisticated in design to provide unusual versatility.

The new Pentax Auto 110, unveiled at the biennial Photokina fair in Cologne, Germany, in September, is a fully automatic SLR that weighs only about 6 ounces and is 3.9 inches long, 2.2 inches high and 1.8 inches deep—one of the smallest SLRs made. Yet it incorporates many features of larger cameras. It accepts interchangeable lenses—normal, wide-angle and telephoto focal lengths are available—and can be fitted with a motor drive that will automatically advance the film.

Among other accessories for the Pentax 110 is a flash unit that automatically sets shutter speed and aperture. A sensor controls the flash so that the correct amount of light is provided for subjects as close as 2½ feet and as distant as 15 feet. A light-emitting diode (LED) in the viewfinder glows green unless the available light is so dim that the shutter has been set automatically to a speed too slow to permit shake-free pictures; then a yellow LED goes on.

The exposure system of the Pentax 110, controlled by a silicon photocell, automatically sets both diaphragm and shutter, which are combined in a single device. It is a leaf shutter that opens only far enough to create the aperture called for. This unit is not built inside the lenses, as the diaphragm is in most camera systems, but is in the camera body, simplifying the problem of providing interchangeable lenses for an automatic camera.

Two new 110s from Kodak, both with built-in flash, are the modestly priced Ektralite and the high-speed Ektramax, which has an f/1.9 lens made with a plastic aspherical element *(pages 144-147)*. The Ektralite, which is meant for simple snapshooting, requires neither focus nor exposure adjustments. On the Ektramax, exposure is set by a four-position "weather dial." Focusing is done by setting the lens to the estimated subject distance.

Agfa-Gevaert demonstrated at Pho-

Agfamatic 901E Motor with Built-in Motor Drive

tokina the first 110 with a built-in, motorized film winder. Once it has been loaded, the Agfamatic 901E Motor advances the film automatically for each exposure—allowing shooting as rapid as two frames per second—and then winds to the end of the roll after the final frame has been exposed.

The Sunpak 2000 E, a sleekly styled camera, is somewhat simpler than the other new models. It has automatic exposure control and built-in electronic flash; the viewfinder flips up for use but will not fold back until the flash has been turned off.

Perhaps the most unusual of the new cameras is the National/Panasonic C-R1: it has a built-in AM radio. As a camera it is simple, having a shutter of fixed speed, a lens of fixed focus and aperture and a built-in flash unit. The radio operates off the batteries that power the flash.

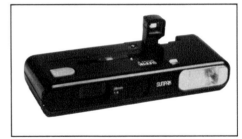

A Flip-up Viewfinder for Sunpak 2000 E

Olympus XA, Dust Sheath Open

Pocketable 35s

Some new 35mm cameras are almost as compact as the 110s *(page 153)*. Small and light, they feature collapsing lenses or sliding dust sheaths that make them easy to slip into pocket or handbag. Two focus themselves.

The 35mm that has a sliding dust sheath is the Olympus XA, a rangefinder camera exhibited at Photokina. Closed, the contoured sheath creates a smooth-surfaced, soft-cornered shape for easy carrying. For compactness, the six-element f/2.8 lens has been designed so that it can be mounted very close to the film plane. The front of the lens does not move during focusing, thus allowing the cover to be closed at any setting. When the sheath slides open, the lens, viewfinder, double-image rangefinder and rear eyepiece window are exposed and the camera is ready for use. After the aperture is adjusted manually, the camera automatically selects the shutter speed.

The XA has two safeguards to prevent common malfunctions. With the matching electronic flash plugged in, setting the aperture control to "flash" automatically sets the lens aperture to f/3.5 and pops up the flash-charge indicator.

When the sheath encloses the camera's vital parts, the battery power automatically switches off and the shutter release retracts into the camera's body.

The Vivitar 35 EM's four-element f/2.8 lens collapses behind a flat protective shield. To flip the shield aside and extend the lens for use, a lever at the base of the camera is moved. The emergence of the lens activates the automatic exposure-control mechanism, which adjusts shutter speed. Focusing is done by setting the estimated distance on the lens ring.

The Ricoh FF-1 also has a lens that

A Pop-Out Lens Hidden in Vivitar 35 EM

folds into the camera body to be protected by a hatch. The body is plastic, reducing the camera weight to about 10 ounces. The Ricoh FF-1 is fully automatic; the CdS-cell exposure meter determines aperture and shutter settings. The f/2.8 Color Rikenon lens is focused with the aid of a distance scale.

Fuji introduced at Photokina the Flash Fujica Auto Focus, a compact 35mm with automatic focusing—a system that remembers. Focusing is provided by the electronic-optical Visi-

tronic device *(Photography Year 1978, pages 86–89)*. Once the shutter release is pressed halfway, the lens is locked in the focus setting. So long as the release is partially depressed, the focus setting is unchanged and the camera remembers while the photographer shifts his angle for the composition he wants.

For automatic focusing in dim light, Fujica's Beam Sensor illuminates the subject enough for the Visitronic device to function. The camera also has a built-in flash, for which correct exposure is set as the lens is focused. For daylight photography, exposure is controlled by a CdS cell that adjusts shutter speed.

The Yashica Auto Focus also has a focusing memory that allows the photographer to shift his angle of view after an automatic system has focused on his subject. The memory operates by a special focus-lock button. Like the Fujica, the Yashica uses the Visitronic autofocus module and has shutter speed controlled by a CdS cell. The shutter locks and an LED flashes when available light is too dim for exposure without flash. The built-in flash pops up to link aperture setting to the lens focus.

Yashica Auto Focus

Canon A-1 with Motor Drive

Automated SLRs

The major technological news in 1978 was made by 35mm SLR cameras of professional quality that are almost completely computerized, with more versatile automatic features than the so-called automatic snapshot cameras *(pages 136–139)*. The Canon A-1 and the Konica FS-1 are the most elaborately fitted out with electronic controls, but other cameras offer many similar features. All come with manual override so that the photographer can disconnect the automatic controls at will.

The Canon A-1 is typical of the new breed. It provides five different modes of operation: full automation for quickest operation, manual selection of shutter speed for action shots, preselected aperture for still lifes and portraits, total manual control and a flash setting. An optional motor drive is available.

Almost as versatile is the Konica FS-1, which includes a built-in motor drive as standard equipment. Automatically advancing the film after each shot, the camera can shoot a frame every .64 second if the shutter release is held down. As the film is rolling, the automatic exposure system meters the scene and sets the diaphragm; the photographer must preselect the shutter speed. Despite the addition of automatic devices, the camera is smaller than other 35mm SLRs with their accessory winders. Size is also kept down by use of a new, compact 40mm f/1.8 lens designed especially for the FS-1.

A newly designed film-winder accessory is a prominent feature of the Chinon CE-3 Memotron. The winder has an electronic circuit that allows the photographer to program the shooting of a variety of sequences. It can operate steadily at two frames per second, shoot series limited to as few as four or as many as 24 frames, make single time-lapse frames at intervals of one to 30 seconds, or simply advance the film automatically, one frame at a time.

The Chinon's automatic exposure system, which adjusts shutter speed after the photographer selects the aperture, will work with almost any screwmount lens, whether or not designed to couple automatically for exposure control. As a result, lenses can be chosen from more then 3,000 different types and focal lengths now on the market.

This unusual advantage is achieved by the use of an extremely responsive light sensor made of two silicon cells. It is sensitive enough to gauge illumination with the lens stopped down to the desired f-stop. Unlike most controls, which measure illumination with the lens wide open, then shift the aperture to the desired f-stop, the Chinon's system measures after the lens is stopped

Chinon CE-3 Memotron

down and the shutter release is pressed, completing operation in the split second before the shutter opens.

The compact Rolleiflex SL35 E has an automatic exposure control that operates with the aperture preselected and remembers the exposure setting. When the photographer depresses the shutter release partway, he locks the exposure selected by the meter, permitting him to shift his angle without changing the settings.

Like the Rolleiflex SL35 E and Chinon CE-3, the new Nikon FE includes a memory-lock exposure control to enable the photographer to aim one way for automatic exposure setting, then partially depress the shutter and shift his angle slightly to shoot the picture. A

Rolleiflex SL35 E Compact, Computerized SLR

1978 accessory for the FE is the Model SB-10 flash, which automatically sets the shutter to ¹/₉₀ second, the correct speed to synchronize with the strobe unit. The SB-10 automatically provides the right amount of light for either of two aperture settings—f/4 or f/8—so that the photographer can select an aperture giving him the depth of field he desires.

The automatic Minolta XG-7 35mm SLR accepts an accessory motor winder that, at 7 ounces, is one of the lightest and smallest available. Despite its size, the winder advances film as fast as two frames per second. The exposure system prevents inadvertent overexposure by locking the shutter release if the shutter speed needed for correct exposure exceeds ¹/₁₀₀₀ second—the maximum. Changing the aperture or switching to manual frees the release.

The shutter release is designed so that a light touch does not release the shutter, but lights the viewfinder indicators that display the automatically selected shutter speed. The XG-7's electronic self-timer warns that the shutter is about to fire by increasing the speed of a blinking light in the last few seconds.

Yashica's FR1, like other automatic SLRs, has viewfinder displays of aperture setting and shutter speed. When set for automatic control, the camera selects shutter speeds ranging from 4 seconds to ¹/₁₀₀₀ second. The camera has an unusual provision for reading the frame counter in dim light: a tiny bulb that serves to test the battery also lights up the numbers.

Made by Yashica, and sharing many parts with the FR1, are two new Contax models, the 137 and 139. Both are compact and automatically controlled by computerized circuits. An unusual scheme adjusts flash output for correct exposure. A silicon cell in the bottom of the camera, aimed at the back of the lens, gauges light from the flash and turns the flash off when sufficient light has entered the lens.

The two Contaxes are nearly identical. The 139 has a shutter that can be manually adjusted to speeds from 1 to ¹/₁₀₀₀ second, while the 137 has only two manual settings. However, the 137 includes a built-in automatic winder that can advance the film as fast as two frames per second; there is no manual film-advance lever.

Yashica FR1, a Camera That Thinks

Canon FD SSC Aspherical 24-35mm Zoom

The New Lenses
A number of unusual lenses were introduced in 1978, including a diversity of zooms, long lenses of special construction and—indicative of a return to the vogue for diffused portraits—soft-focus lenses. The new zooms are made light and compact by special optical design, or by the acceptance of slower speed at their long focal settings.

The first zoom lens with an aspherical element appeared when Canon introduced for its cameras an f/3.5 FD SSC Aspherical, which adjusts from 24mm to 35mm focal length. Taking advantage of the ability of an aspherical element to correct aberrations *(pages 144–147)*, designers produced a lens with only 12 elements—it is 5 inches long and weighs 18 ounces. It does not change length during zooming—the elements shift inside the lens barrel.

At Photokina, Nikon announced the availability for its cameras of the very responsive Zoom-Nikkor f/4, a lens that shifts from 25mm to 50mm with a quarter turn of the zoom ring. It, too, is small—just 4.4 inches in length and 21 ounces in weight.

For Minolta cameras, four compact MD Zoom Rokkor-X lenses were introduced: a 24-50mm f/4, a 35-70mm f/3.5,

Konica 35-70mm Zoom, Controlled by One Ring

a 50-135mm f/3.5 and a 75-200mm f/4.5. For Konica cameras there is a small f/3.5 zoom designed to cover the focal-length range of 35mm to 70mm.

In an unusual approach to reducing size and weight, two zooms for Pentax cameras have smaller maximum apertures at long focal lengths than at short focal lengths. One, for wide-angle coverage, changes from f/3.5 at 28mm focal length to f/4.5 at 50mm; the other is f/2.8 at 35mm and f/3.5 at 70mm.

The same trick of varying speed was employed by Fuji for a lens, presented at Photokina, for its Fujica cameras. Said to be the smallest and lightest zoom—less than 2 inches long and weighing only 10 ounces—it covers the range of 29mm to 47mm, changing from f/3.5 to f/4.2.

Zooms were also manufactured with mounts that fit many 35mm cameras. The Tamron 35-80mm Macro Zoom, like

Minolta's 600mm f/6.3

the zooms from Fujica and Pentax, changes speed, from f/2.8 to f/3.5; it can produce an image one-half lifesize on the film when at its extreme close-up setting. Vivitar's Series 1 24-48mm f/3.8 has three independently moving element groups. The Hoya 25-42mm f/3.5 will focus to within 10 inches.

Among the new long lenses are two that use mirrors to bounce light back and forth as it is focused into an image, giving long focal length in a short barrel. The Canon 500mm f/8 SSC is 5.5 inches long and weighs 26 ounces; it focuses as close as 15 feet—at that

Olympus Super-Fast f/2 21mm

distance a head and shoulders fill the 35mm frame. The Vivitar Series 1 800mm f/11 Solid Catadioptric Telephoto is only 3.3 inches long but has a focal length of 800mm, thanks to mirrors and 10 elements packed tightly to form a virtually solid lens. This dense construction also gives high resistance to shock and temperature extremes.

A Minolta long lens—the 600mm f/6.3 MD APO Tele Rokkor-X—is apochromatic; that is, highly corrected for the chromatic aberration that particularly afflicts long lenses. It achieves this quality with an element made from calcium fluoride crystal, which, unlike

Mamiya's Adjustable Soft-Focus for Portraits

glass, bends all colors of light about equally. An accessory converter doubles the focal length, making the 600mm lens into a 1,200mm lens with a maximum aperture of f/12.7.

Of the short lenses that appeared in 1978, the Zuiko MC Auto-W 21mm from Olympus is among the fastest of the super-wide-angle designs. With a focal length of only 21mm, it has a maximum aperture of f/2.0.

Two lenses designed to create the flattering effects of soft focus, newly returned to popularity for portraits, are available from Minolta and Mamiya. The Minolta 85mm f/2.8 Varisoft Rokkor-X has a four-position adjustment to control spherical aberration, in this way creating a progressive increase in diffusion toward the edges of the frame.

The other new soft-focus lens—the Mamiya-Sekor SF 150mm f/4C—is made for the Mamiya RB67 2¼ x 2¾ SLR used by many portrait photographers. The lens has three interchangeable diffusion discs, each with a different aperture that is surrounded by smaller holes. Each disc provides a different degree of diffusion; with no disc installed, the lens is sharp.

Tiny Sunpak 80 Flash, Shown Near Actual Size

Faster Films

In addition to the high-speed slide film that was introduced by Kodak *(pages 148–152),* several different types of new films were put on the market by German and Japanese firms. These films, mainly made in 35mm sizes, include fast emulsions intended for the production of black-and-white and color negatives, as well as a medium-speed film for color transparencies.

For sale in Europe, Agfa offered Agfacolor CNS 400, a color-print film of very high speed—an ASA rating of 400— and relatively fine grain. It is available in 35mm cassettes.

Fuji introduced two films. One, sold in Japan in 35mm and 120 sizes, is Neopan 400, a high-speed, fine-grained black-and-white film. Rated at ASA 400, it can be pushed three f-stops: it can be exposed as if the rating were ASA 3200, then developed longer than usual to strengthen the image.

Fuji's new slide film, available in Japan in 35mm and 120 sizes and in the United States in the 35mm size, is an improved version of the Fujichrome 100 previously sold. Its speed is ASA 100, and it is said to produce greater sharpness and more brilliant colors than its predecessor was able to.

Flashes for Fast Film

Thanks to the increased light sensitivity of new fast color films *(pages 148–152),* the latest flash attachments can be smaller and more portable, since a less powerful flash is needed. This change is especially evident in the compact, simple attachments priced below $20.

The Sunpak 80, only 1.1 inches tall and 2.3 ounces in weight, delivers ample light for most shots with fast film. It runs on either a single AA battery or a rechargeable nickel cadmium battery. The more elaborate and costly Sunpak 420 has a setting that reduces light output so that it can charge up and fire as fast as four times a second, making it useful with motor-drive cameras. Its adjustable flash head, like those on other Sunpak bounce flashes, can be set to any of 27 positions to bounce light off ceiling or wall.

The Braun Consul 400 can slip into a shirt pocket—it is 4 inches high, 1 inch deep and weighs 4 ounces. Its height lessens the red eye reflections that occur with a flash near the lens.

To reduce battery drain, the Hanimex TB655 Thyristor has an electronic mem-

Flash That Turns Itself Off from Hanimex

Variable-Coverage Vivitar 285 Flash

ory circuit that shuts off power after 40 seconds. Power is restored at the touch of a button. The Hanimex also features a wide-angle attachment, three filters and a bounce head that tilts to six positions. It automatically provides the correct light at either of two f-stops.

The Vivitar 55, like the Braun Consul, has a vertical design to raise the flash away from the camera lens and avoid red-eye pictures. It weighs only 2.7 ounces without its AA batteries, and is 1.5 x 3 x 2 inches in size.

The Vivitar 285 is perhaps the most versatile of the new flash units. It operates automatically for exposures made within 70 feet. The auto-exposure circuits operate at four f-stops. Its light sensor can be removed and aimed separately from the unit—useful when the flash is set off the camera or is bounced. The flash power can be adjusted manually, as is needed often for close-ups. The pattern of light can be made to cover the angle of view of lenses of focal lengths from 28mm to

105mm, while the head will tilt to 90°.

Rollei introduced a new series of four models of Beta flashes. The most expensive, Beta 4, can provide light for correct exposure automatically over a distance as great as 40 feet—even though it is powered by only two AA batteries. It can be used manually or automatically at three f-stops, and its flash head tilts 60° while the automatic-exposure sensor remains aimed at the subject. The head can be fitted with a unique fan reflector that provides diffuse illumination comparable to that created by the reflective umbrellas employed for studio work.

Among other accessories for the Beta 4 are plastic domes that fit over the flash head to give mixtures of bounce and direct lighting. Each dome sends part of the light upward through a top opening to bounce off the ceiling and part of the light forward through a plastic diffuser that lowers intensity in that direction. Two domes provide different degrees of forward diffusion.

Rollei's Beta 4 Flash with Fan Reflector

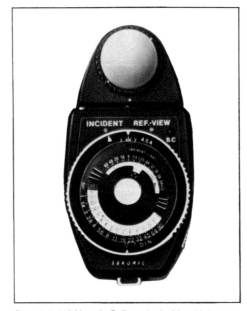

Sekonic L-418 Meter for Reflected or Incident Light

More Readable Meters

Advanced electronics made reading an exposure meter less of a trial in seven 1978 models, all using silicon cells for sensitivity and accuracy. The Sekonic L-418 lacks the usual needles and scales. Instead, its dial automatically rotates to indicate exposure settings when the meter is turned on. Equipped with a swivel head to make aiming more accurate, it can measure light reflected from or falling on the subject. A push button locks in the reading to record it for future reference.

Vivitar brought out four meters that also contain electronic circuits designed for simple operation. All are designed to run on a 9-volt battery, powering a silicon cell that covers 35° of view, and all have LED displays to signal low battery, to warn if light is too bright or dim for measurement and to

indicate that the reading is completed.

The costliest of the new Vivitars, the 260LX, gauges not only available light but also pulsed strobe flashes and the accumulated exposure value of a series of flashes over a period of as long as 90 seconds. Like the Sekonic, it indicates correct aperture-shutter combinations directly—a tiny motor turns the dials in response to signals from the gauging circuits.

The Calcu-Light meter gives readings in numbers displayed in LEDs, which are translated into aperture and shutter settings with the help of a manually operated dial. This meter also measures reflected or incident light, and has a memory system.

To gauge exposure required for critical areas within distant subjects, the Pentax Spotmeter has a pistol-grip and viewfinder. Squeezing the pistol trigger activates a display in the viewfinder, indicating a number that refers to camera settings on a scale.

Pistol-Grip Pentax Spotmeter

Darkroom Aids

A new automatically focused enlarger and a pair of enlarger lenses unlike any that were available previously came on the market in 1978.

The Leitz Focomat V35 Autofocus, available with a color head containing fade-resistant filters, incorporates several improvements that simplify darkroom work. The magnification scale on the arm of the enlarger head and the filter setting knobs are illuminated so that they can be easily read in the dark. To prevent buckling of the negative during printing, the film is kept cool by a heat-reflector mirror in the lamp and an infrared filter.

Among accessories for this enlarger is a timer (lower left in illustration at top) with an unusually wide range. It can time intervals from .1 to 99.9 seconds in .1-second increments and from .01 to 9.99 minutes in .01-minute increments. When used to count minutes, it sounds a warning five seconds before the desired interval is up.

Two new lenses are made by Leitz to work with the V35: the 40mm f/2.8 WA Focotar, which gives from 3 to 16 times magnification; and the Rodenstock Ysaron 50mm f/3.5, which will magnify from 3 to 12 times. Both have illuminated f-stop markings.

Two unique lenses, adaptable to a number of enlargers, came from Computar. A wide-angle 30mm f/2.8 lens for 35mm film gives large magnifications without requiring that the enlarger head be raised a great distance from the easel: it can make a 20-by-30-inch print on an average 35mm enlarger. The lens is designed to be placed the same

Leitz Focomat V35 Enlarger with Color Head

distance from the film as normal lenses, allowing its use with condenser or diffusion enlargers. The fall-off of light at the edges, common with wide-angle lenses, is reduced by coating one of the elements to even out the illumination.

The other Computar lens, the 55mm, is exceptionally fast—f/1.9—for sharp, large prints made from negatives that otherwise would require long exposure times. It uses an unusual solution to a problem that afflicts large-aperture lenses—the difficulty of providing a "flat field" of maximum sharpness from edge to edge at all magnification settings. Computar made one of the elements inside the lens "float" so that it could shift slightly backward or forward

Computar's Fast Lens with Focus Adjustment

with a dial. This adjustment is needed only when the lens is used wide open. After the desired magnification is set and the lens is focused for sharpness at the center of the image, the floating element is shifted until the edges of the image are as sharp as the center.

Miscellany

A new self-cleaning filter removes dirt particles—as small as .0008 inch—from water used for processing, preventing damage to fragile emulsions. The Unitron Universal Water Filter, which fits standard faucets, also has a

Unitron Self-Cleaning Water Filter

valve that reverses the water flow and flushes the filter element clean.

Framed photographs are often hard to view—the glare of the glass obliterates portions of the image. To prevent this glare, a special type of glass has been introduced by Edmund Scientific Co. Instead of the rough surface found on most nonglare glass, the new type, called Denglas, has an antireflection coating similar to those found on camera lenses. The coated glass also is said to screen out ultraviolet rays that cause images to fade.

Discoveries/5

Discoveries/5

JAN STALLER

ARTHUR OLLMAN

RAMÓN AND ANTÓN EGUIGUREN

JOHN PFAHL

Newcomers with a Flair for Color

A quartet whose photographs reflect a worldwide fascination with color and unconventional landscapes makes up this year's group of promising unknowns

The little-known but talented photographers whose work appears on the following pages surfaced during a worldwide search that differed significantly in method from those conducted by *Photography Year* in the past. To locate promising newcomers for each of the previous six issues, the Editors asked a half dozen or so of the leading figures in photography—photographers and critics, educators and editors—to nominate a small number of little-known photographers for recognition in *Photography Year*. But the number of talented people, known and unknown, has increased so dramatically in recent years that it is frequently difficult for the best-informed authority to keep up to date with all of the emerging artists, even within his own special area of interest.

This year the Editors undertook a broader search, using a finer net cast more widely. Instead of seeking formal recommendations from a handful of advisers, the Editors mobilized the staff of Time-Life Books and the international network of bureaus, correspondents and stringers who report for all Time Incorporated publications. In India, Larry Malkin, New Delhi bureau chief, got a name from a Bombay-based photographer who had shot a *Time* cover. Amsterdam correspondent Janny Hovinga went to the organizer of a photography show she earlier had covered. In Hong Kong, *Time* bureau correspondent Bing Wong's list of four names came from a local freelance photographer. In Rio de Janeiro, stringer Alison Raphael not only went to her news sources, but also sent in the name of a local photographer whose work she personally admired.

In all, 200 nominations were submitted by staff members and correspondents in 21 foreign and American cities. The Editors then requested from each nominee a portfolio of up to 25 prints. One photographer was finally tracked down, after a four-week search, taking pictures in the jungles of Colombia.

By the time all 200 submissions had arrived, they filled the long side of a 20- by 30-foot room. Most were mounted prints packed in fiberboard boxes, but some transparencies came in business envelopes, and among other entries were handmade books, triptychs, a custom-designed corduroy pouch containing tiny prints, and a four-foot crate of prints that was delivered by courier in a truck.

In all, 10,000 photographs were reviewed. Most were in color, continuing the trend of recent years, and more were prints than transparencies, indicating the impact on photographic art of the advent of inexpensive home color processing. Also apparent was the increasing popularity of large-format cameras. Street scenes shot from the hip with miniature cameras were rare; more evident were carefully composed 4 x 5 and 8 x 10 views rendered by photographers who are also careful printers. One entrant even revived the platinum process, an expensive printing technique abandoned early in the 20th Century, for his landscapes.

New vogues in subject matter also could be detected. It seems that today's aspiring photographers are more interested in things than people. Trees, fences, parked cars, buildings, walls, dominated the portfolios. Perhaps after two decades during which the camera was used to record fast-moving urban and suburban life, a new generation of photographers, committed more to camera and printing technique than to recording experience on the fly, has turned back to the tradition of still life and landscape.

All four of the portfolios chosen to appear in this year's Discoveries section were in color, and three of them comprised landscapes. Jan Staller *(pages 166-173)* creates inventive twilight photographs that made a lasting impression on Robert Mason, Time-Life Books director of photography; Mason nominated Staller after looking at his portfolio during an interview. Arthur Ollman *(pages 180-189)* produces imaginative, technically astounding night pictures; he was nominated by Jim Enyeart, the newly appointed director of the Center for Creative Photography in Tucson, Arizona. John Pfahl *(pages 190-198)* was nominated by Nathan Lyons, director of the Visual Studies Workshop in Rochester, New York. Pfahl uses a 4 x 5 camera to produce manipulated landscapes that are marked by witty *trompe l'oeil* effects. Antón and Ramón Eguiguren *(pages 174-179)* were among the nominees of the publishing, advertising and fashion sources who were contacted by Bill Lyon, *Time* stringer in Madrid. The Eguiguren brothers, the only Discovery whose subject is the human being, use modern photographic technology to echo the Romantic tradition of their country's art.

Jan Staller— The Light of the City

A 26-year-old Manhattan photographer finds inspiration in the clash of artificial and natural illumination on one subject: an abandoned elevated highway at dusk

After traffic was banned on Manhattan's crumbling West Side Highway in 1973, Jan Staller, a young architectural photographer who lives and works near the roadway's lower end, was one of many nearby residents who slipped through the barriers to take advantage of the open space for strolling, running or cycling. The once-elegant elevated highway was "like a grand promenade," says Staller. It ran for six miles from the financial district's crowded skyscrapers at the tip of Manhattan to midtown, and had unparalleled vistas—the Hudson River and its piers to the west and the island's cloud-scraping skyline to the east. When demolition of the roadway began in the summer of 1977, Staller says, "that was incentive enough for me to decide to photograph it today and figure out what to do with the photographs tomorrow. I stuffed a small tripod and my camera into a small backpack, hopped on my bike and began to make the photographs in this portfolio."

Staller took pictures on and around the highway for more than a year, and the result is an eye-catching series of brilliantly colored urban landscapes. Some scenes capture the interplay of city and river—like the shot opposite of a bright traffic light against the shadowy shapes of ships and piers. A few pictures contrast freshly fallen snow with the city's soot-stained architecture. But more than anything else, Staller's photographs, which he has taken mostly at twilight, capture the intense, clashing hues created as the city's lights begin to come on, and mixtures of incandescent, fluorescent, mercury-vapor and sodium-vapor lighting alter the colors of fading daylight.

For Staller, who was born in 1952 on New York's Long Island, an interest in photography blossomed almost naturally in a home where his father was an avid amateur and his older brother was a professional. He majored in photography at Maryland Institute in Baltimore, and in 1975 moved to New York, where he established himself as an architectural specialist. Staller's professional work, mostly interior shots, has appeared in a number of architectural and interior-design publications.

After experimenting with 35mm and view cameras, Staller settled on the square format of the $2^{1}/_{4}$ x $2^{1}/_{4}$ single-lens reflex. He achieves his unusual color effects by using a professional negative film, Vericolor II, designed for relatively long exposures. Staller extends his exposures beyond the recommended times, shooting at 10 seconds to four minutes, and sometimes he also mixes evening daylight with illumination from incandescent and sodium-vapor street lamps. The result in many cases is a negative that reproduces colors unnaturally. Staller compensates by manipulating filters during enlarging, generally aiming for a more or less natural appearance. His final images measure only eight inches square, but he prints them on an 11-by-14-inch sheet to create a wide white border that both isolates and intensifies the rich hues of his cityscapes.

Martin Street Pier, New York City, 1978

West Side Highway at 23rd Street, New York City, 1978

Manhattan Skyline at Perry Street, 1977

West 23rd Street, New York City, 1978

World Trade Center, New York City, 1977

S.S. John H. Brown II, New York City, 1978

Under the West Side Highway, New York City, 1978

Two Brothers' Old-fashioned Romance

Using hand-painted backgrounds, photomontage and soft focus, the Eguigurens pay tribute to the ideal of their Iberian homeland

The pictures that Ramón and Antón Eguiguren, two brothers in Barcelona, team up to produce are unmistakably Spanish. Not only do most of their colorful images center on a classic Iberian beauty whose ebony hair is pulled back in an Andalusian swirl, but surrounding her are the red capes, roses and accordion-pleated hand fans traditionally associated with romantic Spain. Many of the brothers' pictures are photographic tributes to Spanish painters, and actually look as if they were created with a brush rather than a camera. Both men set out to be painters, and they still regard paintings as a source of inspiration.

When the Eguigurens pay homage to an artist they do not try to reproduce his poses or settings exactly, but rather to reflect "his atmosphere, his world," says Antón. In one such series—a highly romantic studio sequence with vivid hues, a dark background and focus so soft that the model seems to be peering through a gauzy veil (pages 178-179)—the Eguigurens evoke the work of Guilio Romero de Torres, a turn-of-the-century Cordoban painter whose stylized portraits were reproduced on bank notes. In another recent group, the brothers use striking hand-colored photomontages (opposite, and pages 176-177) to create bizarre juxtapositions that are reminiscent of the work of Spanish surrealist Salvador Dali.

Ramón, 33 years old, and Antón, two years younger, are the sons of a prosperous manufacturer from Zumara, a coastal village in the Basque country. They began taking photographs together in their teens. In 1970, to launch joint careers in commercial photography, they moved to Barcelona—Spain's advertising center—hoping to apply their ideas and techniques to fashion and publicity. The conservative Spanish business community was unreceptive, however, so the brothers had to concentrate their most creative efforts on their personal endeavors—although as their reputation as artist-photographers grows, they find commercial clients more amenable to offbeat approaches.

The Eguigurens use a variety of techniques, most of them relatively well-known. The soft-focus pictures—which, like most of their images, use Antón's wife, Maria, as the model and often include painted props—are carefully arranged studio scenes shot through the grease-coated lens of a 35mm camera. For the more ambitious photomontages, the elements—Maria, her cape, the sky, as well as the foreground and background—are each photographed separately on black-and-white film. Prints of these elements are cut apart and pasted together. After being tinted with watercolors, the assemblage is reshot on color film and usually printed as a 12-by-16-inch photograph.

Hand-painted Photomontage, 1978

Photomontage with Hand-painted Cape, 1977

Photomontage with Hand-painted Background, 1977

Spanish Woman, 1975

Woman with Hand-painted Fan, 1975

Arthur Ollman— Glowing Images Out of the Dark

In San Francisco a young photography teacher ignores the limitations of his color negative film to create a series of otherworldly nighttime scenes

An air of eerie unreality permeates Arthur Ollman's cityscapes. Not only do houses, sea walls, park benches and other man-made objects look like architectural models, but grass, trees and other vegetation seem molded out of plastic. Even the sky appears to be a dramatically lit backdrop. Adding to the unsettling atmosphere of these images are colors so unexpected that they seem almost supernatural. Even more surprising, Ollman's brilliantly colored photographs were taken in the middle of the night.

Working between nine at night and two in the morning at sites he has spotted during the day, Ollman photographs a view of California the eye never sees. In faint middle-of-the-night light, he must use exposures that last from 45 seconds to six minutes. To do this successfully, Ollman relies first on instinct. "I see as much with my skin as with my eyes," he says. "I try to feel the next image being near." More important, he employs his deep understanding of the technical idiosyncrasies of color negative film to explore its reaction to very long exposures.

Like all modern color films, the color negative is composed of three layers, one for each primary color. During normal exposures—between 1/10 and 1/1,000 of a second—each layer of the film responds to light in a predictable fashion that gives a balanced representation of natural colors. During exposures like Ollman's— exposures for which the film was not designed—the three layers respond to light in radically different ways. They no longer act together in balance, and the resulting color rendition shifts away from true-to-life values.

Sometimes Ollman will return one element in a scene—usually a neutral surface, such as pavement or sand—to its normal color by adjusting the filters he uses in his enlarger. The rest of the colors in his 16 x 20 prints, however, stray far enough from familiar daytime values to give the viewer the uneasy feeling that he is looking at a synthetic world—an impression that is intensified by the graininess of Ollman's jumbo enlargements.

Ollman, 31, came to this photographic style only in 1977, although he has been photographing seriously since the age of 17. After studying art history at the University of Wisconsin and trying his hand at organic farming in Maine, he moved to San Francisco to concentrate on photography. In addition to pursuing personal work, he now teaches photography at local museums and community colleges.

Divisadero Street Mansion, San Francisco, 1977

Sea Wall, Ocean Beach, San Francisco, 1977

Sunset District, San Francisco, 1977

Water Fountain, San Francisco, 1977

Merry-Go-Round in Rossi Park, San Francisco, 1977

House Wrapped in a Striped Tarpaulin, Chula Vista, California, 1978

Yucca Tree, San Francisco, 1977

House on Seal Rock Road, San Francisco, 1978

John Pfahl—
Bagels
and Rocks

To suggest that the world is not what it seems, a photography professor adds tape, lace and even delicatessen rolls to postcard-pretty landscapes

John Pfahl has long been intrigued by the ambiguities that arise when the three-dimensional world is transformed into the flat, two-dimensional surface of a photograph. In his richly hued images Pfahl, a 39-year-old associate professor of photography at Rochester Institute of Technology, sets out to draw the viewer's attention to this interplay with illusions that are deliberately perplexing. At first sight, a bright yellow angle cutting through a columned portico *(page 198)* or a series of parallel blue dashed lines on the doors of a rustic shed *(page 192)* seem to be graphic designs drawn onto the surface of the photograph. Other pictures contain objects totally extraneous to the setting—the doughnut-shaped rolls called bagels in a waterfront yard *(opposite),* or lace at oceanside *(page 197)*—and they, too, seem to be the result of some addition after exposure. Closer examination, however, reveals that Pfahl performed all of his sleight of hand before he tripped the shutter. The bagels and lace are a real part of the scene, as are other unlikely objects such as pieces of cord and a piepan. And the even more striking lines, angles and other geometric patterns are pieces of tape, rope or aluminum foil stuck to columns, rocks and trees.

Pfahl, who was born in 1939 in New York City and raised in nearby New Jersey, traces his interest in photography to a course he took in 1959 while studying art at Syracuse University. He arrived at his tricked-up scenes when he became involved in color photography. Finding gallery doors shut to color photographs in the early 1960s, he turned to silk-screen printing. Then in 1974, working with a composer of avant-garde music, he began to take color photographs in which bits of tape stuck to the landscape would be the notes in an abstract score. "I became so excited with the visual aspect of the notation and the illusionism that I decided to drop the musical aspects," Pfahl says. He also became fascinated by the dissonance his unexpected additions introduced into postcard-pretty scenes, such as desert moonrises and mountain crags. For the next four years, armed with a "suitcase of ideas" for visual tricks and a car trunk full of rope, tape, lace, plastic balls and other potentially useful objects, Pfahl devoted most of his free time to looking for promising settings—around his home and in a series of trips to such diverse locales as Florida and Utah.

After spotting a setting, Pfahl spends from two to eight hours getting ready. Using a Polaroid attachment on his 4 x 5 view camera, he takes a shot of the landscape. On a sheet of clean plastic placed over this print Pfahl carefully draws in the elements he wants to add. Then, mounting the plastic overlay on the camera's ground-glass viewing screen and using it as a guide, he runs back and forth, making and correcting his additions to the scenery, sometimes checking his progress with more Polaroid exposures. After finally taking the picture on color negative film—and conscientiously removing his additions—Pfahl uses standard darkroom procedures to create 8 x 10 prints reproducing his altered landscapes with such clarity of detail that disturbing clues force the viewer to look twice—and, in keeping with one of art's oldest traditions, to question his own perception.

When the photographer spotted the tires weighing down a tarpaulin over a huge pile of road salt (below), he set out to duplicate their pattern by arranging in the foreground smaller objects of similar shape—round, with a hole in the middle. "I found in researching this project," he says half-jokingly, "that doughnuts were too plump and Life Savers too small." He finally settled on the hard breakfast rolls called bagels.

Bagel Pile, South Buffalo, New York, 1976

One of Pfahl's earliest experiments with geometric
eye-bafflers used pieces of blue tape stuck to the doors
of a rural building. Pfahl arranged the tape strips
to create the illusion that three parallel dashed lines,
aligned with the crossbars on the farthest door,
have been added directly onto the print.

Shed with Blue Dotted Lines, Penland, North Carolina, 1975

In a rubble that had been abandoned by a sculptor, thin black masking tape was attached to the stones. Lines on the ground glass of the view camera served as Pfahl's guide to make the tape —which snakes in three dimensions over the rock contours —form a rectangle in the two-dimensional focal plane.

Pink Rock Rectangle, Lewiston, New York, 1975

These oceanside trees with bands of plumber's foil tape
wrapped around their trunks give the puzzling
impression of being transparent just at the point where
a thin strip of sea appears in the background.
During the three hours that it took Pfahl to set up this
photograph, several groups of bathers arrived,
but all settled down outside the range of the camera.

Australian Pines, Fort DeSoto, Florida, 1977

The only addition to this rugged, mountainous scene was a piece of white cord, which seems to complete the point of a deep cleft. To find this picturesque setting for his visual trick, Pfahl hiked five miles up the Virgin River in Zion Canyon in hip-high water.

Canyon Point, Zion National Park, Utah, 1977

For this photographic in-joke, satirizing the famous
1941 picture by master photographer Ansel Adams of a
moonrise over Hernandez, New Mexico, a piepan
mimics the full moon. Pfahl had to move quickly just at
sundown to get the pan in place on a desert cliff
while there was still light for the aluminum pan to reflect.

Moonrise over Piepan, Capitol Reef National Park, Utah, 1977

Lace pinned along the edge of a coastal bluff makes
a visual pun, simulating the filigree of frothy surf several
hundred feet below. A barely visible beach stroller —
who appears to be almost a part of the cliff's vegetation
near the center — provides a good indication of
the distance between foreground and background.

Wave, Lave, Lace, Pescadero Beach, California, 1978

Yellow tape forms a right angle in the classic colonnade of an art museum near the photographer's home. Although the dashes appear to be the same size, the tape on the column in the foreground was only a few inches long, while the piece on the pavement, at right, measured more than 10 feet.

Yellow Right Angle, Buffalo, New York, 1975

The Year's Books/6

A Poignant Cry / PETER MAGUBANE: *Aftermath of a Train Crash,* 1966

How Women Photographers See Themselves

Mystery and satire, irony and wry humor characterize an unusual anthology of 119 perceptive self-portraits

IN/SIGHTS: SELF-PORTRAITS BY WOMEN. Compiled by Joyce Tenneson Cohen. 144 pages. David R. Godine, Publisher, Boston. Hardbound, $15.00; softbound, $7.95.

The female psyche and the camera as a tool for exploring it—these are the concerns of *In/Sights: Self-Portraits by Women,* a collection of 125 photographs by 66 women photographers, compiled by Joyce Tenneson Cohen over a two-year period. In part a reflection of the feminist movement, with its emphasis on self-discovery, this book is in far greater part a forum for self-expression. In its pages women present themselves as they see themselves, for others to see.

The images are revealing, but scarcely primers for conventional self-portraiture. In attempting to convey elements of their inner selves, these photographers donned masks and costumes, used outrageous props, dipped into collage and montage. They indulged in visual fantasies, as when the editor, herself a photographer, depicted herself as two people meeting in a dreamlike garden *(page 210).* Or they ignored the very heart of portraiture, choosing to show the human face blurred, distorted, partly obscured—or missing altogether.

Thus, one photographer held her camera at arm's length, but focused on a pier behind her; transformed by this treatment, her face becomes a huge, anonymous mask *(page 207).* Another trained her camera on a bleak and banal interior and called the result a self-portrait because the room's emptiness sums up her own identity crisis at the time she shot the picture. And still a third, in perhaps the most poignant self-portrait of all, turned her back on the camera and photographed her aging flesh and gray hair—though the hair, still lively, is caught into a ponytail tied with a jaunty velvet bow *(page 212).*

In creating these portraits, and particularly in solving the problems of how to photograph oneself without being obvious, the photographers used various techniques. Some composed their scenes beforehand, leaving a blank space in the composition for themselves, then set the camera on a timer and entered the picture at the last minute. Others used mirrors or mirrored surfaces as aids. In the portrait at right, a mirrored reflection of the photographer and a child distances the subject from the present time and suggests the past. In another portrait *(page 204),* the photographer's face reflected in the side of a station wagon ironically suggests a role for which she felt herself destined—that of the suburban mother.

The book is given an added dimension by the inclusion in a special section of the photographers' own comments on their work. Some of these quotes have been excerpted for use with the photographs that appear on these pages. But for many of these portraits the image is so powerful and the message so clear that no words are needed. The portrait of the young woman in both dungarees and skirt, one overlaid on the other *(page 205),* scarcely needs words to express the photographer's self-image—as a person in whom "egos and alter egos were freely superimposed and made to coexist."

For a series, including several nudes, that evoked girlhood times in the family attic, Jane Tucker made this looking-glass portrait of herself with a dreaming child. Complicating the image is a second child, also dreaming, curled across the top of the mirror.

JANE TUCKER: *Nudes in the Attic*, 1976

The photographer doing what she loves, photographing, is mirrored in the shiny door panel and the partially raised window of a station wagon holding a mother, a baby and a dog. The portrait contrasts the photographer's career with what she once thought she would become: a suburban housewife.

CHRISTINE PAGE: *The Way I Saw Myself Before Becoming a Photographer,* 1976

To create this humorous vision of an interior self in lacy camisole and skirt, and an exterior self in plaid work shirt and pants, the photographer posed herself twice on the same couch, then made a collage of the result, using part of one print to mask a section of the other.

GILLIAN BROWN: *Alter Ego*, 1976

This photographer sees herself "as a character poking around the edges of the 'all-American fantasy.' " Her self-portrait, as a bobby-soxed tourist hand-in-hand with a friend, was shot at a famous all-American tourist attraction, Niagara Falls.

SUZANNE WINTERBERGER: *Niagara Falls*, 1975

Alone in Boston and looking for good images, Chris Enos held her Nikon at arm's length and left her face out of focus in the foreground of this picture of a weathered pier at low tide. She took the self-portrait because "I was the only person I knew in Boston at the time."

CHRIS ENOS: *Self-Portrait*, 1975

A china swan, a Victorian gown and a shawl are this photographer's devices for gaining insight into the elegant turn-of-the-century world of a grandmother she never knew. "I was examining our similarities and differences—what has been handed down," she writes, "and what perhaps should be discarded."

The hands of a ghostly trio of headless women reach toward the sleeping subject, who for years "disregarded all women as I had disregarded myself." The eerie self-portrait was made by a tripod-mounted camera at the top of the stairs, set on a timer, giving the photographer time to rush down and jump into bed.

HONOR CONKLIN: *Anna's Swan*, 1975

ABIGAIL HEYMAN: *Figures on a Staircase*, 1975

Two black-garbed women—one strolling, one reclining—encounter each other in a leafy garden. The photographer produced this mysterious double self-portrait in the darkroom by printing two negatives on the same piece of photographic paper.

JOYCE TENNESON COHEN: *Self-Portrait,* 1976

"As I thought about it I realized that what I actually had in mind was a self-portrait," says Jane Schreibman (left) of this picture. It was originally planned as a campy send-up of a high-fashion photograph, for which she and a friend posed in a Manhattan loft.

JANE SCHREIBMAN: *The Ladies,* 1977

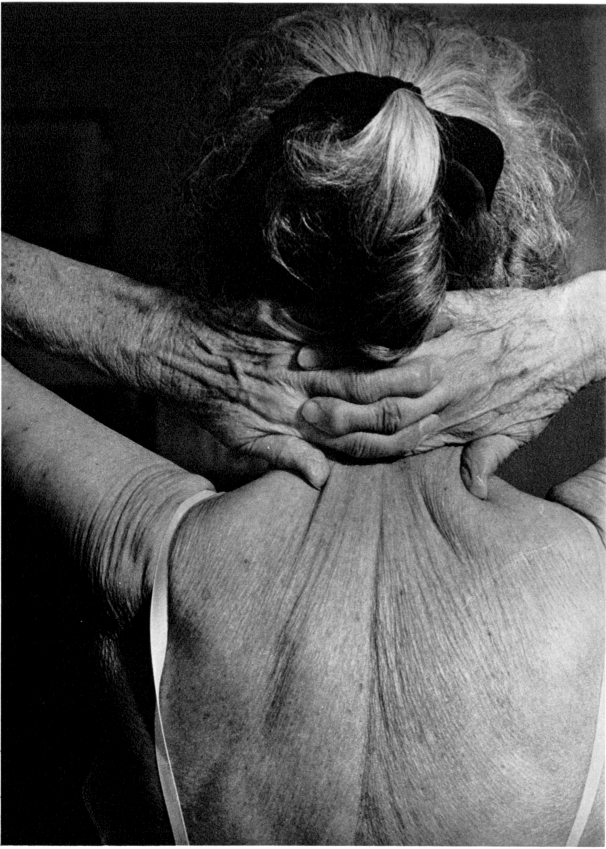

For this powerful self-portrait, the photographer turned her back on a prefocused camera with timer set, and locked her arthritic hands behind her neck, thumbs pressed into her flesh. "Those lines shooting down my back, the curl of my ponytail, the twist in the shoulder strap, the force of my thumbs and thrust of my arms, all communicate something of what I like to consider myself."

NINA HOWELL STARR: *Considering Myself,* 1977

"My presence is totally in the picture," says Hildy Pincus of this strangely melancholy Brooklyn interior where *"an empty couch, the late afternoon light, a portrait of two people, now dead, holding hands,"* offers both a memory of loss and a visual metaphor for the emptiness she felt when the photograph was taken.

HILDY PINCUS: *Self-Portrait*, 1975

A Poignant Cry from the Beloved Country

A gifted black South African photographer earns governmental condemnation and journalistic prizes for haunting images of life in his troubled homeland

MAGUBANE'S SOUTH AFRICA
Photographs and text by
Peter Magubane.
116 pages. Alfred A. Knopf, Inc.
New York. Hardbound, $12.95;
Softbound, $7.95.

"A white policeman pressed the muzzle of a machine gun against my temple threatening to shoot me. I sat praying: for the slightest mistake he could pull the trigger." This harrowing experience was not exactly unexpected to Peter Magubane, a black photographer in South Africa. His disturbing images are the stigmatic symbols of life under the rigid segregation of apartheid.

Magubane's photographs of this Kafkaesque society—in which blacks cannot vote in national elections or even make their homes in cities, but must nevertheless work in them, commuting on overcrowded, poorly maintained trains—appeared first in the African magazine *Drum,* later in the liberal Johannesburg newspaper *Rand Daily Mail.* He was consequently subjected to police beatings, imprisonment in solitary confinement for 586 days and torture (he was forced to stand without sleep for five days on a platform three bricks wide). In 1970, he was "banned" for five years, which meant in effect that he could not practice his profession.

And yet in 1976, immediately following a four-month prison term for taking pictures like the one on page 217, showing black youths carrying a slain comrade during a summer of student rioting, Magubane won South Africa's prestigious Enterprising Journalism Award for some of the very pictures that had led to his imprisonment. It was the first time a black South African had been given the prize.

Magubane was born near Johannesburg 46 years ago and started taking pictures as a schoolboy with a battered box camera given him by his father. In 1955 he went to work for *Drum* as a messenger and spent nights trudging the streets of Johannesburg experimenting with a 2¼-by-2¼ camera purchased for him by the magazine's photo editor. By the time he joined the *Daily Mail* in 1965, Magubane was an accomplished news photographer whose pictures captured with uncompromising clarity the anguish of South Africa in the faces of its blacks, mixed-ancestry "coloreds" and Asians.

Not all of *Magubane's South Africa* is painful: a piano teacher beams as her pupil bursts into song *(page 223)* and laughing women pass a bemused baby through the air with upraised hands at a church festival *(page 221).* But most of this book is as grim and bitter as the face of the old woman opposite, whose gangster grandson, a product of South Africa's slums, had just been ordered executed. On page after page the scenes are of rioting, humiliation and death.

To capture such pictures Magubane has had to put aside his shock and become, in his words, "a feelingless beast." He has also had to be clever. Once he hid his camera in a hollowed-out loaf of bread. And when menaced by police while photographing child laborers on a farm near Johannesburg, he pointed warningly to the moving needle of his light meter. "It is transmitting everything you say to us here back to our office," he said. He and his reporter companion were quickly released.

This old woman, her bitter face framed in the crumbling window of her home in Soweto, a black slum outside Johannesburg, is the grandmother of Boy Sevenpence, a criminal who terrorized Soweto in the 1950s and had just been condemned to execution when this photograph was taken.

A girl and boy in their Sunday best exchange glances during a kindergarten picnic at the Johannesburg Zoo. When the picture was made, in 1966, the zoo was open to blacks only on certain days. Even today blacks, Asians and "coloreds" must use separate facilities.

Three youths carry the body of a friend killed by police moments earlier during the 1976 rioting that left more than 100 blacks dead in shantytowns ringing the white cities. After taking this picture, Magubane was forced at gunpoint by the police to leave the area.

Faces fixed in grief, mourners flank caskets that hold 30 of the 69 victims of the Sharpeville massacre—a bloody 1960 clash that occurred when blacks in Sharpeville, about 25 miles from Johannesburg, protested against a hated apartheid law forbidding them to travel away from their homes without passbooks.

Two boys who, Magubane notes, "looked only about 14" rest on metal cots at a Johannesburg employment center for blacks. They had been brought into the city by labor contractors from tribal areas around the country to work in South African mines and farms; such recruits are selected for their strength.

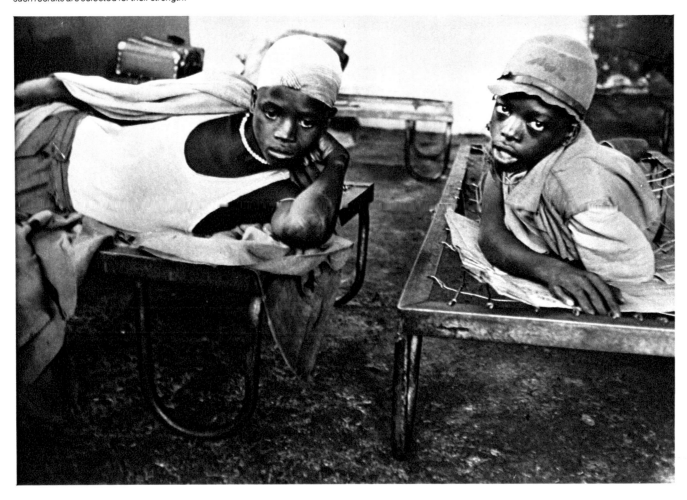

A girl stares in bewilderment while her grandmother adjusts a kerosene lamp hanging inside a tent — their new home in a resettlement district that had been set up by the South African government.

In the Transkei, a nominally independent black "homeland" in the southeast portion of South Africa, a wide-eyed infant is passed hand to hand over the heads of a throng that has gathered at a church festival to celebrate the memory of a female faith healer who had died many years before.

A domestic tragedy is recorded differently on the faces of twin brothers whose mother was killed in a car accident on Christmas Day, 1975. Magubane, who saw the accident, visited the family the following day to get this picture. The boy on the right, comments Magubane, "was hard; he really wouldn't shed a tear."

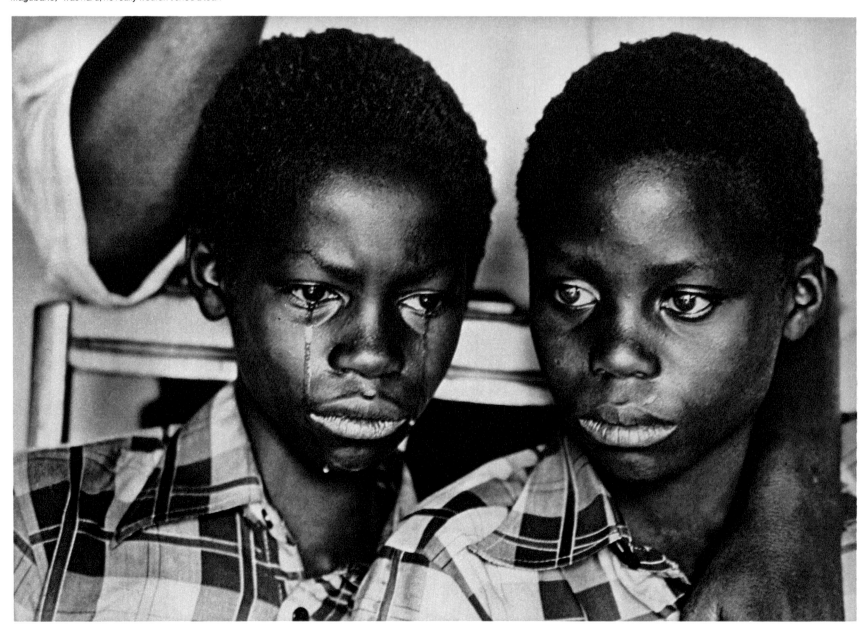

Putting depth of field to artful use, Magubane photographed a smiling music teacher as a soft and shadowy, supportive presence behind the sharper image of her enthusiastic young student. The picture was made in 1956, the year after Magubane's career was launched with a photographic assignment from the South African magazine Drum.

Other Books

The editors recommend the following additional photography books published during 1978.

Current Work

AVEDON: PHOTOGRAPHS 1947–1977

Essay by Harold Brodkey. Farrar, Straus & Giroux, New York. Unnumbered pages. 162 plates. Hardbound, $50.00. Fashionable clothes, and the fashionable people who wear them, by a master photographer.

A BOOK OF PHOTOGRAPHS FROM THE COLLECTION OF SAM WAGSTAFF

Gray Press, Inc., New York. 144 pages. 143 plates. Softbound, $15.00. One man's collection of 19th and 20th Century photographs.

COURT HOUSE: A PHOTOGRAPHIC DOCUMENT

Edited by Richard Pare. Horizon Press, New York. 256 pages. 358 plates. Hardbound, $35.00. The interiors and exteriors of courthouses all over the United States, documented by 24 photographers (*page 47*).

THE ENGLISH

By Ian Berry. Penguin Books, Middlesex, England. Unnumbered pages. 100 plates. Softbound, £2.95. Comic Britannia by an award-winning British photographer.

HIMALAYAN PILGRIMAGE

Photographs by Ernst Haas. Text by Gisela Minke. The Viking Press, New York. 184 pages. 140 photographs. Hardbound, $45.00. The people and landscape of Tibet, photographed in color by the noted photojournalist.

THE LAST AND FIRST ESKIMOS

Photographs by Alex Harris. Text by Robert Coles. New York Graphic Society, Boston. 159 pages. 87 plates. Hardbound, $19.95. Documentary photographs of Alaskan Eskimos, and snapshots by the Eskimos themselves, accompany text by a renowned child psychiatrist.

MARIE COSINDAS: COLOR PHOTOGRAPHS

Essay by Tom Wolfe. New York Graphic Society, Boston. 143 pages. 60 plates. Hardbound, $45.00. Portraits and still lifes on Polacolor film.

MOMENTS: THE PULITZER PRIZE PHOTOGRAPHS

Edited by Sheryle and John Leekley. Introduction by Dan Rather. Crown Publishers, Inc., New York. 128 pages. Hardbound, $12.95. A collection of great news pictures shot between 1942 and 1977.

RECENT DEVELOPMENTS

Photographs by Elliott Erwitt. Introduction by Wilfrid Sheed. Simon and Schuster, New York. 128 pages. Softbound, $9.95. Humorous pictures of animals and people.

RUSSELL LEE, PHOTOGRAPHER

Text by F. Jack Hurley. Introduction by Robert Coles. Morgan and Morgan, Inc., Dobbs Ferry, New York. 207 pages. Hardbound, $25.00; softbound, $15.95. Industrial workers and rural life in the United States and abroad, as seen by one of America's best documentary photographers.

SKREBNESKI PORTRAITS: A MATTER OF RECORD

Pictures and introduction by Victor Skrebneski. Doubleday and Company, Inc., Garden City, New York. Unnumbered pages. Hardbound, $27.50. Portraits of celebrities.

Historical

THE AMERICANS

Photographs by Robert Frank. Introduction by Jack Kerouac. Aperture, Inc., Millerton, New York. 184 pages. 83 plates. Hardbound, $25.00. A reprint of a Swiss photographer's classic profile of Americans in cafés, public places and on the road in the mid-1950s.

THE COLLECTION OF ALFRED STIEGLITZ: FIFTY PIONEERS OF MODERN PHOTOGRAPHY

By Weston J. Naef. Metropolitan Museum of Art/The Viking Press, New York. 530 pages. Hardbound, $30.00. A selection of turn-of-the-century masterpieces from Stieglitz's private collection, with historical information.

EDWARD STEICHEN

Introduction by Ruth Kelton. Aperture, Inc., Millerton, New York. 96 pages. Hardbound, $7.95. A selection of 41 legendary photographs, from turn-of-the-century soft-focus portraits to crisp architectural studies of the 1920s.

THE FACE OF CHINA, 1860–1912: AS SEEN BY PHOTOGRAPHERS AND TRAVELERS

Preface by L. Carrington Goodrich. Historical commentary by Nigel Cameron. Aperture, Inc., Millerton, New York. 159 pages. Hardbound, $25.00.

FLASHBACK! THE 50s

By Eve Arnold. Alfred A. Knopf, New York. 149 pages. Hardbound, $12.95. Coverage of personalities and events by a well-known photojournalist.

GREAT PHOTOGRAPHIC ESSAYS FROM LIFE

Edited with commentary by Maitland Edey. New York Graphic Society, Boston. 278 pages. Hardbound, $24.95. Twenty-two of the magazine's famous picture essays, reproduced as they originally appeared.

IMPERIAL CHINA: PHOTOGRAPHS 1850–1912

Text by Clark Worswick and Jonathan Spence. Foreword by Harrison Salisbury. Pennwick Publishing Inc., New York. 151 pages. Hardbound, $22.50. Two books of portraits, architectural views and street scenes from China by European and American photographers.

JESSIE TARBOX BEALS: FIRST WOMAN NEWS PHOTOGRAPHER

By Alexander Alland Sr. Camera/Graphic Press Ltd., New York. 191 pages. 183 photographs. Hardbound, $25.00. The life and work of a gifted photojournalist whose pictures appeared in major newspapers and magazines in the first half of the century.

MINOR WHITE: RITES AND PASSAGES

Biographical essay by James Baker Hall. Aperture, Inc., Millerton, New York. 144 pages. 143 plates. Hardbound, $25.00. A selection of landscapes, interiors and portraits by the late editor-photographer-teacher.

MOHOLY-NAGY: FOTOS UND FOTOGRAMME

By Andreas Haus. Schirmer/Mosel, Munich. 252 pages. 150 plates. Hardbound, DM 68. (Distributed in the U.S. by Light Impressions Corporation, Rochester, New York. Hardbound, $40.00.) Photograms, portraits and city views by a photographer-member of the German design center of the 1920s, the Bauhaus.

PHOTOGRAPHY IN AMERICA: THE FORMATIVE YEARS 1839–1900

By William Welling. Thomas Y. Crowell Company, New York. 431 pages. Hardbound, $29.95. A history of the first 60 years of American photography, illustrated mainly by photographs not previously published.

RUSSLAND: 1904–1924

By Eric Baschet. Swan Verlag, Kehl am Rhein. 279 pages. Hardbound, DM 69. Personalities and events from the tumultuous period of the Bolshevik revolution in Russia.

STEICHEN: THE MASTER PRINTS, 1895–1914: THE SYMBOLIST PERIOD

By Dennis Longwell. Museum of Modern Art, New York. 180 pages. 73 plates. Hardbound, $35.00. The catalogue of the 1978 exhibition devoted to Steichen's early gum-bichromate and platinum prints.

SUDEK

By Sonja Bullaty. Introduction by Anna Farova. Clarkson N. Potter, Inc., New York. 192 pages. 80 plates. Hardbound, $25.00. Limited Edition, $45.00. Landscapes, portraits, panoramas and surrealist fantasies from the 50-year career of the late Czech master.

WALKER EVANS: FIRST AND LAST

Harper and Row Publishers, Inc., New York. 203 pages. 219 plates. Hardbound, $29.95. More than 200 photographs—some never before published—from the great American's 45 years in photography.

Technical

ALTERNATIVE PHOTOGRAPHIC PROCESSES

By Kent E. Wade. Morgan and Morgan, Inc., Dobbs Ferry, New York. 179 pages. Softbound, $11.95. Step-by-step instructions for creating photographic images on materials other than the usual paper, such as glass and metal.

CAMERAS: FROM DAGUERREOTYPES TO INSTANT PICTURES

By Brian Coe. Crown Publishers, Inc., New York. 240 pages. Hardbound, $15.95. Historical development of the camera from 1839 to the present, illustrated with color and black-and-white drawings.

DARKROOM 2

Edited by Jain Kelley. Lustrum Press, New York. 160 pages. Softbound, $17.50. A discussion of methods for making prints by 10 photographers.

EISENSTAEDT'S GUIDE TO PHOTOGRAPHY

By Alfred Eisenstaedt. The Viking Press, New York. 176 pages. Hardbound, $17.95. Instructions in picture-taking from the famed *Life* photographer, with illustrations from his own work.

THE GUM BICHROMATE BOOK: CONTEMPORARY METHODS FOR PHOTOGRAPHIC PRINTMAKING

By David Scopick. Light Impressions Corporation, Rochester, New York. 88 pages. Softbound, $7.95. How to make hand-coated pigment prints using a 19th Century process.

Critical

DOROTHEA LANGE: A PHOTOGRAPHER'S LIFE

By Milton Metzer. Farrar, Straus & Giroux, New York. 399 pages. Hardbound, $15.00. The biography of a photographer famous for her depiction of rural America during the Depression.

GRANTS IN PHOTOGRAPHY: HOW TO GET THEM

By Lida Moser. Amphoto, New York. 112 pages. Hardbound, $12.50. A survey of sources of funds available to groups or individuals in the United States (*page 41*).

THE VALIANT KNIGHTS OF DAGUERRE: SELECTED CRITICAL ESSAYS ON PHOTOGRAPHY AND PROFILES OF PHOTOGRAPHIC PIONEERS

By Sadakichi Hartmann. Edited by Harry W. Lawton and George Knox. University of California Press, Berkeley and Los Angeles. 364 pages. Hardbound, $25.00. Essays and biographical sketches, published between 1898 and 1913 by one of photography's earliest and most influential critics.

Roundup/7

Roundup/7

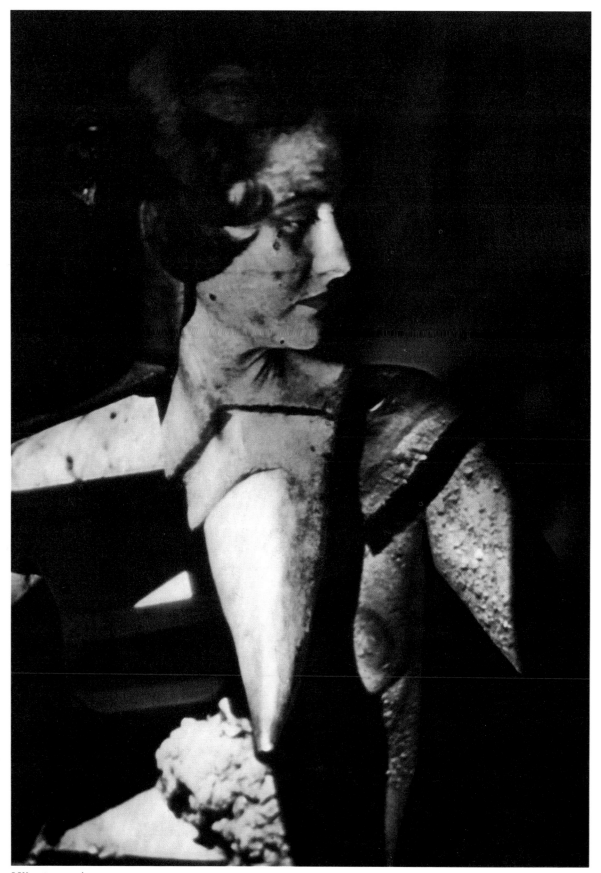

Milestones / ARTHUR S. SIEGEL: *Portrait of Barbara*, 1948

The Man Who Found Heroes Everywhere

Gene Smith, himself possessed of uncompromising courage, revealed the nobility and bravery of celebrities and unknowns alike in classic photographs

After surviving close calls with death in the line of duty, famed photojournalist W. Eugene Smith died at 59 on October 15, 1978, from head injuries suffered in a fall in a grocery store. The irony of his death, in Tucson, Arizona, where he was a professor at the University of Arizona's Center for Creative Photography, was matched by the irony of his life. Few others in his profession created as many heroic images and memorable essays as Smith did during his 42 years as a photojournalist. Yet he was almost as famous for his quarrels with editors as for his pictures.

Born in Wichita, Kansas, in 1918, Smith started free-lancing for local papers while still in high school, and after a few months at Notre Dame, he worked as a staff photographer for both *Newsweek* and *Life*. Then, while working as a combat photographer in the Second World War, he found his true subject matter: obscure but heroic people struggling against adversity. His pictures of the agonies and deaths of soldiers and civilians in the Pacific quickly positioned him among the handful of top war photographers.

In 1945, while photographing at Okinawa, Smith was so badly wounded that he could not work again for two years. When he recovered, he had trouble adjusting to peacetime journalism. He produced such masterpieces of the photographic essay as "Country Doctor" *(page 233)* and "Spanish Village," *(page 232)* but he balked at routine assignments. His last staff assignment for *Life* was a picture essay on the African hospital founded and run by the Alsatian physician-musician-missionary Albert Schweitzer *(opposite)*. Smith felt that a story on Schweitzer's complex personality and work required more than the 12 pages the editors allotted it, and when the essay was printed at that length, he resigned.

After 16 years during which he won three Guggenheim Fellowships, taught photography, published a book and exhibited, Smith went to Japan in 1971 for his last great work of photojournalism, the Minamata essay. Minamata was the story of a small village of Japanese fishermen, many of whom had been disfigured—some even killed—by the effects of industrial pollution. The essay included the celebrated photograph reproduced on page 230, a classic that quickly detached itself from the story to become a permanent part of the modern imagination.

Minamata was the quintessential expression of Smith's refusal merely to interpret events in an interesting and informative manner. He wanted to create ideal images, so true and powerful they would persuade people to abandon war, greed and self-interest. These high expectations led him to extraordinary feats of identification with his subjects, but they also left him perpetually dissatisfied with his results and made the practical accommodations required by any form of journalism difficult—eventually impossible—for him to bear.

In a revealing portrait, Smith captured both the heroic dedication and the driving authoritarianism of Albert Schweitzer, whose work as a missionary doctor in Africa helped win him the Nobel Peace Prize in 1952. Smith, as fanatical a worker as Schweitzer, spent five days and five nights in the darkroom to achieve the dramatic contrasts and subtle details of this photograph.

Man of Mercy, 1954

*Widely known as "the Minamata Pietà," this somber
study of a Japanese mother tenderly bathing her
deformed 16-year-old daughter was the climactic
picture in Smith's celebrated essay on industrial
pollution. Chemical waste dumped into local fishing
waters had contaminated fish eaten by the mother
when she was pregnant, causing her daughter to suffer
a progressively crippling disease.*

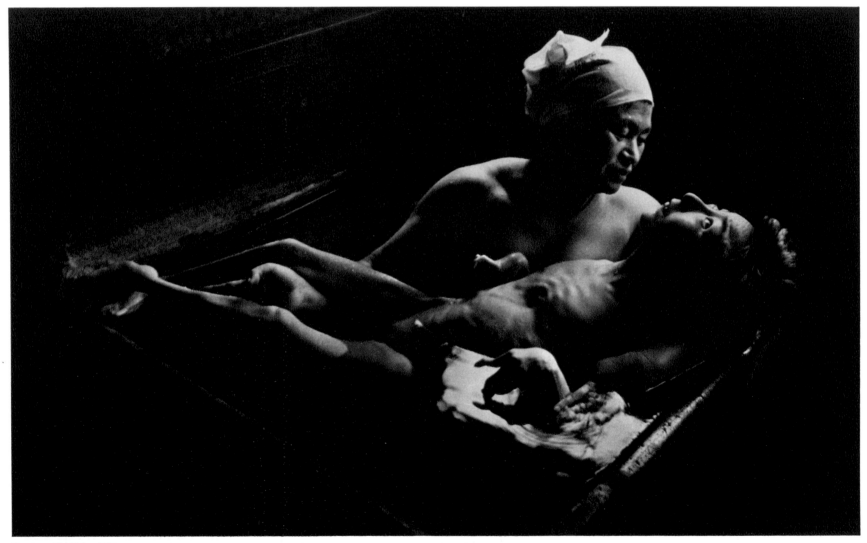

Tomoko and Her Mother, 1972

Burial at sea was the grim fate of many American
sailors during World War II, much of which Smith spent
alongside fighting GIs in the Pacific theater.

Burial at Sea, 1944

*Jagged silhouettes and watchful eyes dominate
this picture of rural policemen from Smith's 1951 essay,
"Spanish Village," which evoked the harsh, sullen
atmosphere of the dictatorship then in power in Spain.*

Guardia Civil, 1951

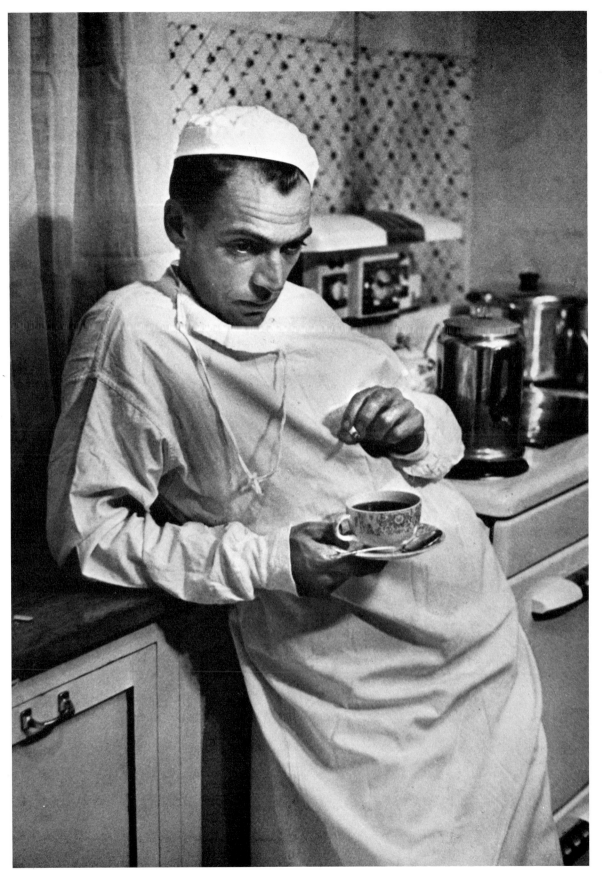

Late at night, after a long day of house calls and
hospital work, the only physician in an isolated Western
ranching community broods over a cigarette and a
cup of coffee. "Country Doctor," the essay from which
this picture comes, won Smith widespread critical
acclaim as well as the gratitude of thousands of general
practitioners, who saw their own lives reflected in it.

After Midnight, 1951

Roundup

Milestones

graphing in such a sanctuary that she was approached by the group of lost terrorists, who asked her for directions and then shot her.

Gail Rubin 1938-1978

Gail Rubin, 39, an American specializing in nature photography, was taking pictures of wildlife on a beach near Haifa, Israel, when she was killed in March by Palestinian terrorists who had landed there by mistake, thinking they were near Tel Aviv. She had first gone to Israel in 1969 on a three-week vacation, but was so captivated by the country that she remained there for nine years, working as a freelance photojournalist and writer.

Most recently, she had been photographing species of wildlife mentioned in the Bible, many of them now found only in preserves. It was while photo-

Tsutomu Watanabe 1908-1978

The death of journalist Tsutomu "Ben" Watanabe in January in Tokyo deprived the Japanese photographic community of one of its most respected critics and friends. In 1947, Watanabe became chief editor of *Sekai Gaho* (World in Pictures), an influential Japanese magazine of photography and design. In this capacity he was among the first of his countrymen to combine photographs for storytelling purposes.

The author of four books and the photographic illustrator of others, Watanabe also helped found the Tokyo College of Photography in 1958; he taught there from 1961 to 1969.

Arthur S. Siegel 1913-1978

One of the first photographers of his generation to use color photography as an artistic medium, Arthur S. Siegel died in Chicago in February at the age of 64. "Color," he said in 1954, "is the newest frontier of photography, and like all frontiers it offers thousands of stimulating and exciting challenges."

For Siegel the challenges were rewarding. In 1950 *Life* published seven pages of his color photographs. In 1977 he participated in the Chicago Museum of Contemporary Art's "The City and the Photographer." His work appeared in one-man and group shows as well, and in numerous museum collections.

Siegel also played a prominent part in the education of several generations of American photographers. He started out as a sociologist-photographer who combined teaching with a photojournalist's career. In the 1940s his documentary and news pictures were widely published. But he was increasingly drawn to abstract work, and in 1946 was appointed by designer-photographer László Moholy-Nagy to head the photography program of the Institute of Design at the Illinois Institute of Technology in Chicago, then the center of avant-garde photography in America.

To this period in Siegel's career belongs the portrait of his first wife, Barbara, reproduced on page 227. Siegel made the portrait by projecting a slide onto the subject's face and body before photographing her on transparency film; a dye transfer made from the transparency was exhibited in Siegel's first one-man show, at the Art Institute of Chicago, in 1954.

GAIL RUBIN: *Sea Gull in Israel*, 1976

Karel Hajek 1900-1978

Czechoslovakian photographer Karel Hajek, who died in Prague in March, was a streetcar motorman who became a professional photographer in 1932 when he stopped the streetcar he was driving to take pictures of an automobile accident. For this dereliction of duty he lost his job with the trolley line, but the pictures won him a place on the staff of a Prague publishing house.

During a career that spanned a tumultuous period in European affairs, Hajek covered significant moments in modern history. His pictures of the Nazi invasions of Czechoslovakia in 1938 and 1939 were widely reproduced around the world, as were his photographs of the Nuremberg trials following World War II.

Franco Pinna 1925-1978

Franco Pinna, who died in Rome in April of a heart attack at age 52, was the only photographer that the Italian film director Federico Fellini always welcomed on his set. The color photographs Pinna took during the making of such Fellini movies as *The Clowns* and *Casanova* were widely published in magazines around the world, and were collected in two books. It was Pinna who created the famous portrait of Fellini with half his face made up as a clown *(page 32)*.

Before working for Fellini, Pinna was a photojournalist traveling for top magazines, among them *Life, Paris-Match, Stern, The* London *Sunday Times Magazine* and *Look*. Before that, when he was still in his twenties, Pinna collaborated with an Italian ethnologist, Er-

KAREL HAJEK: *Woman and Child*, Egypt, 1958

nesto de Martino, to produce the illustrations for a series of books on the poor and primitive regions of southern Italy.

Himself a native of a small island off the coast of Sardinia, Pinna was a sensitive observer of Italian life. His quiet, unobtrusive way of working with shy and suspicious people enabled him, as Fellini said on the occasion of a 1975 exhibition in Bologna, "to capture with acute perception the mortal silence, the heartbreaking abandon, the fossilized immutability of certain realities of our country."

Victor Hasselblad 1906-1978

When American astronauts went to the moon, they carried with them cameras designed and made by Swedish inventor Victor Hasselblad, who died in May in his hometown of Gothenburg.

Born into a family of amateur photographers, Hasselblad became interested in bird photography when he was still in knee pants. Between 1923 and 1925 he studied camera design and manufacture at Kodak Pathé in Paris, Zeiss Ikon in Germany and Eastman Kodak in the United States.

During World War II the Swedish air force assigned him the task of developing and manufacturing high-precision aerial cameras. After the War he used this experience to produce a precision, lightweight but very rugged 2¼ x 2¼ single-lens reflex camera with interchangeable lenses. Equipped with interchangeable film magazines as well, the Hasselblad camera permitted the photographer to change lenses and film with ease.

Priced at $400 when it was first put on the market in 1948, the Hasselblad camera was too expensive for most beginners, but it enjoyed great success among professionals and advanced amateurs. Then, in 1962, Hasselblad was awarded a contract by the National Aeronautics and Space Administration to supply cameras to be used during manned space flights.

During one space walk in 1966, astronaut Michael Collins dropped his Hasselblad, which floated away; it is still in orbit around the earth. But the deeply impressive photographs made on these flights—including Frank Bor-man's world-famous and widely reproduced view of earthrise seen from the moon—are the best memorial to Hasselblad's genius.

Otto Steinert 1915-1978

Guru and guide to a generation of German photographers following World War II, Otto Steinert of the University of Essen died in March at the age of 62. He was an electrifying teacher whose educational activities were an integral part of his work as a photographer.

A physician by training, Steinert gave up medicine when he was 33 years old to devote himself fulltime to photography. During the next 30 years Steinert helped lead German photography out of the sentimentality and heroics of the Nazi years and into the mainstream of European art.

In addition to formal teaching, he built notable collections of prints, edited books and staged exhibitions—among the most famous was "Subjective Photography," organized in 1951 for the State School of Arts and Crafts in Saarbrücken. A survey including more than 700 photographs, it familiarized its German audiences with the largely suppressed works of prewar German-based photographers such as László Moholy-Nagy and Herbert Bayer, and contemporary foreigners such as Brassaï and Robert Doisneau of France and the American Man Ray.

Steinert's own photographs made extensive use of darkroom manipulation: solarization, photomontage and negative printing. But whichever technique he employed, Steinert always brought a spare formality to his pictures, a quality

OTTO STEINERT: *Industrial Landscape in the Saarländ,* 1950

displayed in the lean lines and angles of the 1950 print reproduced above. In this picture, a solarization, the pale sky turns dark, black power lines become white and a thin white line edges the top of the building.

Clarence H. White Jr. 1907-1978

Clarence H. White Jr., a photographer who was best known as an educator, died in March. From 1949 until his retirement in 1972, White headed the photography program at Ohio University in Athens, Ohio.

White began his career in photography education shortly after the death in 1925 of his famous father, who was one of a group of early-20th Century American photographers known as the Photo-Secessionists. As a member of the faculty at the photography school that had been founded by his father in New York

City, White attempted to build a bridge between the purely esthetic approach of the Photo-Secessionists and the demands of commercial photography.

Eduardo Hernandez Toledo
1916-1978

Guerrilla warfare was the ultimate subject matter for Cuban press photographer Eduardo Hernandez Toledo, who died in Miami in April at 61 after a long career. Hernandez was best known for his 1958 movies of the Castro revolution, but he also had covered the Sergeants' Revolt that in 1933 brought to power the government Castro overthrew, and he went on to cover attempts by various rebel groups to bring down the Castro regime.

Hernandez began his professional career in 1948 as a cameraman for a Cuban newsreel company, and soon acquired a reputation as a daredevil capable of covering any story regardless of its dangers.

For his coverage of Castro's guerrilla activities, Hernandez packed cameras, film and equipment into the mountains, dodging government troops to reach Castro's insurgent forces. He spent four months traveling with, and photographing, them. The film that resulted, *Sierra Maestra,* was exhibited throughout Latin America to raise money for the rebels, and forced Hernandez to go into exile in Miami.

After Castro's victory the photographer returned to Cuba, but soon grew disillusioned with the new leader and went into exile once again, covering anti-Castro guerrilla activities for the Spanish-language magazine *Bohemia,*

EDUARDO HERNANDEZ TOLEDO: *Shenandoah Junior High School,* Miami, 1977

first from Miami and then from Venezuela. From 1976 to 1978 he was chief photographer for the Spanish-speaking edition of *The Miami Herald,* for which he made such pictures of the city's Cuban colony as the one above.

Roundup

Miscellany

Boston Fire Fighters in 1919, One of Many New Prints from Old Negatives

Soviet Honors for Ansel

For his 76th birthday, on February 20, 1978, Ansel Adams, the dean of American landscape photographers, had a special party thrown in his honor by photography lovers in the Soviet Union. The celebration, which was attended by leading Soviet photographers, artists and critics, as well as U.S. embassy officials, was the climax of a four-week Moscow exhibition of 84 prints by Adams—the first exhibit in the U.S.S.R. ever to feature the work of a single American photographer.

Adams's majestic landscapes and powerful nature studies attracted some 100,000 visitors to the exhibition, drew high praise from the Soviet press and were the subject of a television program. The Moscow Committee of Graphic Artists, which hosted the show, enrolled Adams as an honorary member—a tribute never before accorded a foreign photographer.

New Prints from Old Glass

Capitalizing on the collecting boom in old photographs, two Boston dealers began marketing new prints from old glass negatives. Caroline Gates and Cherie Tripp, both 29, first sold prints during the Bicentennial year from a pushcart near Boston's Faneuil Hall.

Beginning with a few dozen pictures of Boston street scenes, sailing ships, steam locomotives and daredevil balloonists, Gates & Tripp amassed more than 5,000 prints, some made from early negatives borrowed from collectors and historical societies. Recently the firm bought 350 glass plates made by Orville C. Rand, a turn-of-the-century Boston photographer who specialized in such vignettes of city life as the view, above, of the Boston Fire Department in action. By the end of 1978, the firm had turned its cartful of nostalgia into a $150,000-a-year enterprise.

Berkey v. Kodak

On June 16, a federal court in New York City ordered the Eastman Kodak Company to pay $87 million in damages and legal costs to Berkey Photo, Inc., which operates processing plants in New York and eight other states, and is both a customer and competitor of Kodak. Berkey's suit was one of the few successful antitrust cases in the history of the photographic industry, and the damages were among the largest antitrust judgments ever awarded.

Berkey had charged that Kodak monopolized the amateur camera and film markets and unfairly sold film, paper and photochemicals to its own photofinishing division at prices lower than those charged to outside companies

Muscovites at the Ansel Adams Exhibit

Color-enriched Man in the Shroud

like Berkey. In addition to granting the huge monetary redress, the court ordered Kodak to furnish, if requested, photographic paper without the Kodak name on it and to make "identical disclosures" of new research to outside photo processors that it gives its internal photo-processing arm.

Kodak said it would appeal.

Christ in Color?

Venerated by some as the burial garment of Jesus and denounced by others as a medieval forgery, the Holy Shroud of Turin—a linen cloth 14 feet long bearing what appears to be the faint image of a crucified man—has been an object of controversy ever since it first appeared in France 600 years ago. But during a rare public display in Turin in August the famed relic attracted a great deal of photographic attention.

After removal from the bullet-proof case in which it was displayed at Turin's cathedral, the relic was photographed by scientists using special cameras. Their pictures will be analyzed by computers over the next two years, and may reveal details that will help the scientists verify the origin of the shroud and explain how its enigmatic image was formed.

More spectacular, however, was a picture of the shroud billed by the Italian magazine *Oggi* as "the first color photograph of the Christ of the Holy Shroud." *Oggi*'s startling illustration at left, which is highlighted by streaks of bright red, transforms the shroud's ancient sepia-toned imprint into an eerie color image of a suffering face.

The color was totally artificial, introduced into a black-and-white photograph electronically, using a technique developed to create synthetic color for satellite pictures of earth. By means of a computer-controlled device, a black-and-white image is converted by a special type of television camera into electrical signals that represent distinct shades of gray; each shade of gray is then arbitrarily assigned a hue by the operator—he can make any tone in the picture any color he chooses. Finally the color-coded electrical signals are converted into colored light, as in a color-television receiver, and the light exposes a piece of 35mm color film.

While such electronic tinting gives no hint of true color, it does separate tones that might be indistinguishable in black and white, making apparent details that otherwise could be missed. For the Oggi illustration, physicians who have examined the shroud image—and who believe it was formed by a man who had been dead for several hours—guided architect Clino Trini Castelli in the color synthesization.

A Stamp for Photography

Photography received major tribute on a minor scale on June 26, 1978, when the United States Postal Service issued the first American postage stamp honoring the medium. Rather than reproduce an already existing photograph, postal authorities commissioned Ben Somoroff, a New York City photographer known for his studio work, to come up with a new picture. Somoroff's solution: a still life featuring a vintage 4 x 5 view camera *(below)*.

Photography USA 15c

First U.S. Stamp to Honor Photography

Shore's Lily Pads in a Monet Garden

Carter's Cabinet on Film

Photography, it seemed, was about to cross a new threshold when President Carter urged his Cabinet members and other Presidential appointees to use photographs for their official portraits instead of the traditional oil paintings. Joan Mondale, Washington's semiofficial champion of the arts, took charge of finding the talent.

Early in 1978, 15 well-known photographers sent portfolios to Washington for the officials to select from. Not surprisingly, the list included traditional portraitists Arnold Newman, Marie Cosindas and Eva Rubinstein; less predictable were photojournalists Mary Ellen Mark and Jill Krementz, and a pair of photographers, Judy Dater and Jack Welpott, whose work is more often seen on museum walls than along government corridors.

By midsummer, an enthusiastic Jill Krementz had snapped her first photographs of Transportation Secretary Brock Adams, Defense Secretary Harold Brown and HEW's Joseph Califano. What sold the three on Krementz was her idea for the portraits: each would be a montage composed of several prints.

After this impressive beginning, however, the project lost momentum. Official response to Mary Ellen Mark's color pictures of Agriculture's Bob Bergland was delayed and rumored to be negative. Arnold Newman's date with Interior Secretary Cecil Andrus was put off. Polaroid artist Marie Cosindas' first shooting date with Commerce Secretary Juanita Kreps was pushed back six weeks. By year's end, none of the portraits had been completed—not even those for which shootings were finished—and the project seemed threatened by some Cabinet members' lack of interest, bureaucratic red tape and the peripatetic habits of both photographers and officials.

A Photographer in Monet's Gardens

When the Metropolitan Museum of Art in New York City opened an exhibition of 81 paintings by French impressionist Claude Monet in April, the first pictures visitors saw were not Monet paintings but large, richly detailed color photographs. Displayed in a separate introductory gallery, the 18 prints vividly set the stage for Monet's canvases, a group painted during the 43 years Monet lived and worked in Giverny, a village 40 miles northwest of Paris.

The photographs, by Stephen Shore, an American photographer best known for his scenes of American cities, were commissioned by the museum to document the restoration of the Giverny gardens. The gardens—designed by Monet himself—inspired his famous series of paintings of water lilies. They fell into ruin after Monet's death in 1926, and languished until a grant several years ago made it possible to re-create much of their former glory. The restoration prompted the exhibition.

In photographing this enchanted landscape, Shore used color negative film in an 8 x 10 view camera to record the gardens as they exist now. On several occasions he duplicated the viewpoint of Monet's paintings, but most subjects he captured in his own fashion; one is a panorama of drooping willows, another a close-up *(above)* of a water lily floating on a cloud-reflecting pond. Though the photographs were intended to do no more than serve as a prelude to Monet's masterpieces, one museum official acknowledged that Shore's meticulous prints "transcended the functional, so that people left the exhibit remembering them."

Two Dice in 3-D

A gold-framed circle of glass that appears empty at first, but when rotated displays a three-dimensional view of a pair of dice *(below)*, contains within its shimmering depths 1978's bestseller in the young art of holography. Produced by entrepreneur-holographer Don C. Broadbent as a novelty, the dice-patterned pendant went on sale at New York City's Museum of Holography in 1978. The pendant appears blank until it is tilted to reflect light from a certain angle. At that point two dice materialize, showing different faces as the pendant is turned.

To project a three-dimensional image under almost any lighting condition, the dice were recorded on glass that had first been coated with dichromated gelatin emulsion. In most holograms that use this gelatin base, the image is enveloped in a haze of false colors—a problem that is particularly noticeable when the subject to be viewed contains sharp black and whites, as it does here. To achieve the color control that made his illusional dice pay off, Broadbent used a formula, developed after two years of experimentation, that he keeps secret.

Frederick (left) and Arthur Gandolfi with Hand-crafted Cameras

Last of the Hand-made Cameras

When the March 12, 1978, edition of *The* London *Sunday Times Magazine* described the craft of camera makers Frederick and Arthur Gandolfi, the brothers' firm received a flood of telephone calls and letters from prospective clients ordering large-format view cameras. For the Gandolfis, both in their seventies, are the last people anywhere in the world still producing wooden cameras made completely by hand. When they close their business, the craft itself probably will vanish.

The Gandolfi brothers have been satisfying camera customers since 1932.

Holographic Pendant's Dice Can Be Invisible

A Slight Tilt Reveals Two Sides of the Dice

Additional Tilting Produces 7 and 11

Firemen Battling the Eastman House Blaze

Today their clientele consists mainly of advertising photographers, who prize Gandolfi cameras for their lightness—they are half the weight of comparable metal view cameras—and for their special features. Camera collectors who are not photographers also value the matchless workmanship and the materials from which the cameras are made.

Teak and mahogany are used for the frame, brass for the polished fittings. Except for the bellows, lens, and a few knobs and screws, the Gandolfis cut and shape all parts themselves, relying on equipment from another era. Frederick, for example, trims wooden planks down to 1/16 inch—the thickness needed for the joints of a film holder—with a hand-built motor saw he adapted from a Victorian treadle wheel.

Because each camera is different, the Gandolfis do not set uniform prices, but a customer can expect to pay more than $500 for the plainest model. The prices are modest, however, compared with what Gandolfi cameras will probably fetch once the brothers retire.

Strengthened Copyright Act

As authors of "pictorial works," photographers are benefiting from a new U.S. copyright law effective January 1, 1978. Passed by Congress in 1976 after 14 years of debate, the law guarantees a photographer ownership of reproduction rights to his copyrighted pictures for his lifetime plus a single term of 50 years; previously, copyright protection was limited to 56 years.

Also, the new law states more clearly the respective rights of publishers and freelance contributors. In particular, a publisher can no longer assume the full rights to a commissioned work. Rather, free-lancers retain the right to reproduce and distribute photographs taken on assignment unless they agree otherwise in a written contract.

Close Call for a Treasure House

On May 29, 1978, a spectacular blaze erupted in a concrete storage vault at the International Museum of Photography in Rochester, New York, and threatened the museum's $120 million photographic collection, considered to be the world's greatest.

The vault contained more than 3,000 reels of old movie negatives, all on the highly flammable nitrate base used for professional motion pictures until after World War II. The film exploded in flames that quickly spread to two other outbuildings on the museum grounds. A wooden barn housing one of the museum's most valuable properties—18 insulated packing crates containing traveling exhibitions of 19th and 20th Century photographic masterpieces—burned to the ground, but Rochester fireman Barrie Youngblut manned a forklift to save the two-ton treasure.

When hastily gathered museum staffers unpacked the 600 prints inside the rescued crates, they found that only five were destroyed—although the lost five included a Eugène Atget view of a Paris park, valued at $2,500, and a Nevada landscape by Edward Weston.

The blaze never touched the mansion of Kodak's founder, George Eastman, where the bulk of the museum's collection is stored. As a tribute to the fire fighters whose skill prevented serious damage, the museum staged a special three-week exhibit of photographs the firemen rescued—and pictures taken during the near-disaster.

Bibliography

Avedon, Richard, "Munkacsi," *Harper's Bazaar,* June 1967.

Bajuk, D. J., "Computer Controlled Generation of Rotationally Symmetric Aspheric Surfaces," *Optical Engineering,* September-October 1976.

Barr, C. R., J. R. Thirtle and P. J. Vittum, "Developer-Inhibitor-Releasing (DIR) Couplers in Color Photography," *Photographic Science and Engineering,* March-April 1969.

Barry, Les, "The Legend of Sid Grossman," *Popular Photography,* November 1961.

Beaton, Cecil, and Diane Buckland, *The Magic Image.* Little, Brown and Company, 1975.

Bunnell, Peter C., "Clarence H. White Jr., 1907–1978," *Exposure,* Summer 1978.

Capa, Cornell, ed., *The Concerned Photographer 2.* Grossman Publishers, 1972.

Editors of the Foundation Center, *Foundation Grants to Individuals.* The Foundation Center, 1977.

Freytag, Heinrich, "Professor Dr. Otto Steinert," *Camera,* May 1978.

Galleries: A Guide to Washington Art Galleries, November 1978.

Goldsmith, Arthur, "Second Coming I and II," *Popular Photography,* November 1978.

Hanson, W. T., Jr., "Forty Years of Color Photography," *Photographic Science and Engineering,* November-December 1977.

James, T. H., ed., *The Theory of the Photographic Process.* Macmillan Publishing Co., Inc., 1977.

Kingslake, Rudolf, ed., *Applied Optics and Optical Engineering.* Academic Press, 1969.

Lewis, Eleanor, ed., "W. Eugene Smith: Forty Years of Experience," *Darkroom.* Lustrum Press, 1977.

Malinowsky, J., "Contemporary Problems of the Theory of Photographic Sensitivity," *Photographic Science and Engineering,* July-August 1974.

Moser, Lida, *Grants in Photography: How to Get Them.* Amphoto, 1978.

Munkacsi, Martin, "Think While You Shoot," *Harper's Bazaar,* November 1935.

Osman, Colin, *Creative Camera International Yearbook 1977.* Coo Press Ltd., 1978.

Pare, Richard, ed., *Court House.* Horizon Press, 1978.

Price, William H., "The Photographic Lens," *Scientific American,* August 1976.

Smith, Aileen and W. Eugene, "Minimata, Japan: Life Sacred and Profane," *Camera 35,* April 1974.

Sturge, John M., ed., *Neblette's Handbook of Photography and Reprography.* Van Nostrand Reinhold Co., 1977.

Szarkowski, John, *Mirrors and Windows: American Photography Since 1960.* The Museum of Modern Art, New York, 1978.

Tucker, Anne, "Photographic Crossroads: The Photo League," *Afterimage,* April 6, 1978.

"Underexposure," *Newsweek,* April 30, 1978.

"Why the Black Ink is Spurting at Magazines," *Business Week,* December 12, 1977.

Wilson, Ian, *The Turin Shroud.* Victor Gollancz Ltd., 1978.

Acknowledgments

The index was prepared by Jane B. Whipple. The editors also thank:

In the Americas—Ruth Ansel, *The Sunday Times Magazine, New York City;* Conrad Bieber, William Leatherman, *Polaroid Corporation, Cambridge, Massachusetts;* Harry Bowers, *San Francisco Institute of Art;* Peter Bunnell, *Princeton University, Princeton, New Jersey;* Woodfin Camp, *New York City;* Renato Danese, Cathy Gauss, *National Endowment for the Arts, Washington, D.C.;* Merle Deardorf, *L. F. Deardorf & Sons, Chicago;* Charles Desmarais, *Chicago Center for Contemporary Photography;* Caroline Despard, *Smithsonian magazine, Washington, D.C.;* John Dominis, *Sports Illustrated, New York City;* Mary Dunn, *People, New York City;* Jim Enyeart, *Center for Creative Photography, Tucson;* Wendy Ewald, *Appalshop, Inc., Whitesburg, Kentucky;* William Ewing, Ann White, *International Center of Photography, New York City;* David Finn, *Ruder and Finn, Inc., New York City;* James Graham, Frank Kent, George Massios, William Price, *Eastman Kodak Company, Rochester, New York;* John Grimes, *Institute of Design, Illinois Institute of Technology, Chicago;* G. Ray Hawkins, *G. Ray Hawkins Gallery, Los Angeles;* Mrs. Eduardo Hernandez, Luis Hernandez, *Miami;* Brent Herridge, *Children's Photographic Workshop, Salt Lake City;* Evelyn Hofer, *New York City;* Geoffrey James, *The Canada Council Photography Program, Ottawa;* Wayne Karmosky, *Cultural Council Foundation, New York City;* Nancy Kaufman, *Creative Artists Public Service, New York City;* Norman Kleber, *New York City;* Edward Miller, Manuel Ramirez, *Centro de Orientacion & Servicios, Ponce, Puerto Rico;* Lida Moser, *New York City;* Patrick Nagatani, *Venice, California;* Mickey Phleger, *San Francisco;* Bob Pledge, *Contact, New York City;* Marc Pokempner, *Chicago;* Abe Rezny, *Brooklyn, New York;* Fred Ritchin, *New York City;* Susan Rosenberg, Tom Sherman, *Delaware Art Museum, Wilmington;* Mrs. Estelle Rubin, *New York City;* Marcia Schiff, *Polaroid Foundation, Cambridge, Massachusetts;* Max Schwartz, *American Telephone and Telegraph Co., New York City;* Melvin L. Scott, *Life, New York City;* Mrs. Irene Siegel, *Chicago;* Aaron Siskind, *Providence, Rhode Island;* Charles Stainback, *Visual Studies Workshop, Rochester, New York;* William Stapp, *National Portrait Gallery, Washington, D.C.;* Nina Subin, *Esquire, New York City;* Alan Teller, Jerry Zbiral, *Public Art Workshop, Chicago;* David Travis, *Art Institute of Chicago;* Anne Tucker, *The Museum of Fine Arts, Houston;* Lesley Valdes, *Miami;* Thea Weiser, *Quest, New York City;* Robert Wolf, *Henry Street School, New York City;* Sue Wymelenberg, *Boston.*

In Europe—Pierre Barbin, *Paris;* Georges Bardawill, Lyliane Boyer, *Le Nouveau Photocinéma, Paris;* Dr. Walter Boje, *Leichlingen, West Germany;* Nick Callaway, *Galerie Zabriskie, Paris;* Clino Trini Castelli, *Color Terminal, Milan;* Lanfranco Colombo, Beppe Preti, *Il Diaframma—Fotografia Italiana, Milan;* Maria Teresa Contini, *Gabinetto Fotografico Nazionale, Rome;* Mario Cresci, *Matera, Basilicata, Italy;* Sue Davies, *Photographers' Gallery, London;* Michel Decron, *Photo Magazine, Paris;* Pierre de Fenoÿl, *Centre National Georges Pompidou, Paris;* Jacques de Potier, Roger Thérond, *Paris-Match, Paris;* Ger Fiolet, *Gallery Fiolet, Amsterdam;* Piero Berengo Gardin, *Rome;* Aleksandr Gerinas, *Photo Division of the Union of Soviet Artists, Moscow;* Anna-Maria Greci, *Rome;* Professor L. Fritz Gruber, *Photokina, Cologne;* David Halliday, *Film Workshop, Edinburgh, Scotland;* Janny Hovinga, *Amsterdam;* Ian Kellagher, *Edinburgh, Scotland;* Guy Knoché, *Association des Gens d'Image, Paris;* Robert Kroon, *Geneva;* Jean-Claude Lemagny, *Bibliothèque Nationale, Paris;* Valerie Lloyd, *London;* Bernd Lohse, *Bergisch-Neunkirchen, West Germany;* Paola Mina, *Fotolgram, Università di Milano, Milan;* Yevgeniya Mokletsova, *Union of Soviet Journalists, Moscow;* Jean-Luc Monterosso, *Paris;* Michel Nuridsany, *Le Figaro, Paris;* Klaus op ten Höfel, *Agfa-Gevaert Foto-Historama, Leverkusen, West Germany;* Bernard Perrine, *Ecole des Beaux-Arts, Marseilles;* Umberto Pizzi, *Rome;* Heiner Riebesehl, *Spectrum Galerie, Hanover, West Germany;* Christiane Roger, *Société Française de Photographie, Paris;* Wilhelm Schürmann, *Galerie Schürmann und Kieken, Düsseldorf;* Bogdan Turek, *Warsaw;* Peter Turner, *London.*

In Asia and the Far East—Australian Center for Photography, Melbourne; Australian Visual Arts Board, *Melbourne;* Terry Duckham, *Camera and Cine, Sydney;* Jehengir Gazdar, Larry Malkin, K. K. Sharma, *New Delhi;* Mirka Gondicas, *Athens;* David Rubinger, *Jerusalem;* Professor Y. Ernest Satow, *Kyoto City University of Arts, Kyoto;* Robert Slater, *Jerusalem;* Bing Wong, *Hong Kong.*

In Africa—Robert Denton, *Michaelis School of Fine Arts, Cape Town.*

Picture Credits

Credits from left to right are separated by semicolons, from top to bottom by dashes.

COVER—Ramón and Antón Eguiguren; Gjon Mili.

Trends: 11: Linda G. Rich, East Baltimore Documentary Photography Project. 13: Harry Mangual. 14: Carmen G. Santos. 15: Antonio L. Zayas. 16: Carmen G. Santos. 17: Edwin Santiago. 18, 19: Rico Santiago, courtesy Henry Street School, Henry Street Settlement; Alex Martinez, courtesy Henry Street School, Henry Street Settlement. 20: Bonnie Capps. 21: Pam Brashears. 22: Donna Ray. 23: Andrea McCline. 24, 25: Ralph Mitchell. 27: *Life* Magazine, October 1978, © 1978 Time Inc. Reprinted with permission. Photograph by David Deahl—Eddie Adams from Wide World Photos. 29: Copyright © 1978 by the New York Magazine Company, Inc. Reprinted with the permission of the *New York* Magazine. 30: Ghislaine Morel from GAMMA, Paris. 31: Jean-Claude Woestland and Bertrand Rindoff-Petroff (ANGELI, Paris), courtesy *Paris-Match* Magazine; Diana H. Walker—Sonia Moskowitz. 32: Manfred Bockelmann, courtesy *Bunte* Magazine—Franco Pinna, courtesy *Euro* Magazine. 33: Jay: Leviton-Atlanta, courtesy *People Weekly* Magazine; Neil Leifer, Copyright © 1978 Time Inc. All rights reserved—Slick Lawson. 34: Daniel Angeli, from *Eva Express* Magazine, August 12, 1976. 35: George Spitzer (DENIS TARANTO, Paris); Ron Galella—Daniel Angeli, courtesy *Paris-Match* Magazine; Ron Galella. 36: David Hume Kennerly and UPI *(upper right)*, courtesy *Paris-Match* Magazine. 37: Steve Schapiro from SYGMA; Dieter Klar, courtesy *Bunte* Magazine—Patrice Habans from SYGMA, Paris, courtesy *Annabella* Magazine. 42: George Krause. 43: Steven Lojewski. 44: Steve Sprague. 45: Left, courtesy of The United States Geological Survey Archives (2); right, Rephotographic Survey Project (2). 46: Robert Adams. 47: Geoff Winningham. 48: Siggen Stinessen.

The Major Shows: 51: Luiz Carlos Felizardo. 53: Bill Owens. 54: By permission of the estate of Irwin Klein, copied by Paulus Leeser, courtesy of The Museum of Modern Art. 55: Robert Rauschenberg, *Kiesler, 1966*, offset lithograph, printed in color, comp: 33¹⁵/₁₆ × 22″. Collection, The Museum of Modern Art, New York. John B. Turner Fund. 56: Polacolor print by Marie Cosindas. 57: Paul Caponigro. 58: Garry Winogrand. 59: Roger Mertin, courtesy of the Light Gallery. 60: Kenneth Josephson. 61: Linda Connor. 63: Martin Munkacsi from the *Berlin Illustrated News*. 64, 65: Courtesy of the Martin Munkacsi Estate. 66: Courtesy *Harper's Bazaar* Magazine, Copyright © 1933. 67: Courtesy *Harper's Bazaar* Magazine, Copyright © 1935. 68: Courtesy of the Martin Munkacsi Estate. 69:

Courtesy *Harper's Bazaar* Magazine, Copyright © 1934. 70, 71: Courtesy *Harper's Bazaar* Magazine, Copyright © 1937. 72: Courtesy *Harper's Bazaar* Magazine, Copyright © 1934. 73: Courtesy *Harper's Bazaar* Magazine, Copyright © 1938. 63 through 73: Copied by Scott Hyde. 75: Ricardo Malta. 76: Sara Facio. 77: Sandra Eleta. 78: Odilón de Araujo. 79: María E. Haya (Marucha). 80: Pedro Meyer. 81: Antonio Carlos S. d'Ávila. 82: Sara Facio. 83: Rogelio López Marin (GORI). 85: Aaron Siskind, courtesy IMP/GEH. 86: Clemens Kalischer from Image Photos. 87: Max Yavno, courtesy G. Ray Hawkins Gallery. 88: Ted Tessler. 89: Walter Rosenblum, copied by Allen Newbourn. 90: Gloria Nardin Watts, copied by Allen Newbourn. 91: Sidney Kerner. 92: Eliot Elisofon, copied by Scott Hyde. 93: Ralph Steiner, copied by Allen Newbourn. 94: Rudy Burckhardt. 95: Walter Rosenblum. 96: Sid Grossman, printed by Allen Newbourn. 97: Lou Stoumen. 99: Tom Shuler. 100: Timo Pajunen. 101: Pierre Cordier. 102: Mark Klett. 103: By permission of the Trustees of Amherst College. 104: Société Française de Photographie, Paris-Chimanski. 105: Frank Gohlke. 106: John Wood. 107: Copyright © Michael Bishop 1978. All rights reserved. 108: Kaveh Golestan.

The Annual Awards: 111: David Alan Harvey, © National Geographic Society. 113: Yoshikazu Minami. 114: Gerry Cranham. 115: *Suburban Trib* Photo by Michael Wirtz. 116: Hajek-Halke, copied by Photo Reger, Munich, courtesy Cornelia Boje. 117: Willi Moegle. 118: Eddie Adams from Wide World Photos. 119: Leslie Hammond. 120, 121: Josef Koudelka from Magnum. 122: Shigeo Gocho. 123: Dean Conger © National Geographic Society. 124, 125: Alain Chartier. 126: Dr. Doranne Jacobson, © National Geographic Society. 127: Sergei Smirnov, *Izvestia*, Moscow. 128: John Blair. 129: Gisèle Freund. 130: J. Ross Baughman for Wide World Photos.

The New Technology: 133: Neil Montanus, courtesy Eastman Kodak Company. 136: Courtesy Zeiss-Ikon, Stuttgart. 137: Courtesy Eastman Kodak Company—courtesy Agfa-Gevaert, Foto-Historama, Leverkusen—courtesy Tokyo Kogaku (Topcon), Tokyo—courtesy Konica Camera Co. 138: Top and middle courtesy Konishiroku, Tokyo—Konica Camera Co. 139: Courtesy Konishiroku, Tokyo (2)—Evelyn Hofer (overlay by Forte, Inc. courtesy Konishiroku, Tokyo). 140: Courtesy Polaroid Corporation. 141: Fil Hunter. 142, 143: Fil Hunter, drawings by Nick Fasciano, courtesy Polaroid Corporation. 145: Drawing by John Drummond, courtesy Eastman Kodak Company. 146:

Courtesy Eastman Kodak Company. 147: Courtesy Eastman Kodak Company—courtesy Vivitar Corporation—courtesy Canon U.S.A., Inc., drawings by Forte, Inc. 148, 149: John Neubauer. 151: Courtesy Eastman Kodak Company, chart by Forte, Inc. 152: Left, John Zimmerman (2), right, Evelyn Hofer (2). 153: Courtesy Asahi Optical Company, Ltd., Tokyo; courtesy Agfa-Gevaert, Leverkusen— courtesy Berkey Marketing Companies. 154: Courtesy Olympus Camera Co.—courtesy Vivitar Corporation—courtesy Yashica Co., Ltd., Tokyo. 155: Courtesy Canon U.S.A., Inc.; courtesy Chinon Corporation of America. 156: Courtesy Rollei of America; courtesy Canon, Amsterdam—courtesy Yashica, Inc. 157: Courtesy Konica Camera Co.; courtesy Bell & Howell-Mamiya Company—courtesy Olympus Optical Co.—courtesy Minolta Corp. 158: Courtesy Berkey Marketing Companies; courtesy Vivitar Corporation—courtesy Hanimex (U.S.A.) Inc. 159: Courtesy Copal Corp. of America—courtesy Rollei of America Inc.; courtesy Pentax Corporation. 160: Courtesy Ernest Leitz Wetzlar GMBH, Wetzlar—courtesy E.P.O.I., Inc.—courtesy Burleigh Brooks Optics, Inc.

Discoveries: 163: Jan Staller; Stephen M. Gillis—Ramón and Antón Eguiguren; John Pfahl. 167 through 173: Jan Staller. 175 through 179: Ramón and Antón Eguiguren. 181 through 189: Arthur Ollman. 191 through 198: John Pfahl, courtesy of the Robert Freidus Gallery and the Visual Studies Workshop Gallery.

The Year's Books: 201: From *Magubane's South Africa* by Peter Magubane. Copyright © 1978 by Peter Magubane. Reprinted by permission of Alfred A. Knopf, Inc. 203 through 208, 210 through 213: From *In/Sights: Self-Portraits by Women*, compiled by Joyce Tenneson Cohen. Copyright © 1978 by Joyce Tenneson Cohen. Reprinted by permission of David R. Godine, Publisher. 209: Abigail Heyman from Magnum. 215 through 223: From *Magubane's South Africa* by Peter Magubane. Copyright © 1978 by Peter Magubane. Reprinted by permission of Alfred A. Knopf, Inc.

Roundup: 227: Arthur Siegel. 229: W. Eugene Smith for *Life*. 230: Collection of the Center for Creative Photography. 231: W. Eugene Smith. 232, 233: W. Eugene Smith for *Life*. 234: Gail Rubin. 235: Karel Hajek. 236: Professor Dr. Otto Steinert. 237: Courtesy *El Miami Herald*. 238: Courtesy Gates and Tripp Gallery—Nikolai Bolotin. 239: Clino Trini Castelli—courtesy U.S. Postal Service. 240: Stephen Shore. 241: Hick Wells/*The Sunday Times Magazine*, London—Fil Hunter. 242: Wide World Photos.

Index

A numeral in italics indicates a photograph or drawing of the subject mentioned.